Impossible Prophecies

Fulfilled

That Defy Skeptics

COLIN D. STANDISH &
RUSSELL R. STANDISH

Copyright © 2008
Colin D. Standish

Cover design and layout by
Greg Solie • AltamontGraphics.com

Text editing and layout by
Harvey Steck

All emphasis in quotations added by
the authors unless otherwise indicated.

Published by
Hartland Publications
PO Box 1, Rapidan, VA, 22733 USA
(540) 672-3566
Printed in the USA

ISBN 978-0-923309-10-7

Contents

1. The Existence of an All-Knowing God........................5
2. Sodom and Gomorrah..9
3. Nineveh, the Doomed City.................................14
4. A King's Dream...20
5. Four Beasts, Ten Horns, and a Little Horn................30
6. A Ram and a He Goat......................................35
7. The Papal Deadly Wound...................................45
8. An Eight-Word Question and the Fate of a Nation..........56
9. The Fall of Communism....................................61
10. Babylon, the City Which Cannot Be Rebuilt...............73
11. Jerusalem, the Eternal City?............................82
12. Messianic Prophecies of Christ's Birth and Ministry.....90
13. The Years of Christ's Ministry and Sacrifice Foretold..101
14. Old Testament Prophecies of the Capture, Trial, Torture, Crucifixion, Resurrection, and Ascension of Christ.........113
15. What About Unfulfilled Prophecies?.....................123
16. Yet-to-Be-Fulfilled Prophecies.........................131
Index..139
Hartland Publications Book List............................143
About the Authors..159

CHAPTER 1
The Existence of an All-Knowing God

ATHEISTS, skeptics, agnostics, and evolutionists all have something in common. They either deny the existence of God or, alternatively, deny that we can prove or defend the existence of God. Obviously, God foresaw that many members of the human race would come to such conclusions. Therefore, in His revelation through the sacred oracles of Scripture, God chose to reveal in remarkable detail many of the events which would transpire through the future course of human history. These details are so explicit, so easily comprehended, that those who choose to study them will find the greatest assurance of the handiwork of the One who is the Creator of the universe, the One who is all-knowing, the One who comprehends the beginning from the end. This is the claim recorded three times by the Apostle John in the book of Revelation.

> I am Alpha and Omega, the beginning and the ending, saith the Lord, which is, and which was, and which is to come, the Almighty. (Revelation 1:8)

> And he said unto me, It is done. I am Alpha and Omega, the beginning and the end.... (Revelation 21:6)

> I am Alpha and Omega, the beginning and the end, the first and the last. (Revelation 22:13)

God has chosen to verify His mighty foreknowledge through prophecies which no limited human mind could ever have detailed with such pinpoint accuracy. John was supremely confident that he, along with Peter and his brother James, had seen Christ transfigured (glorified by the Father) in the presence of Elijah and Moses, who had been taken to heaven by God. He had heard the voice of God declaring that Christ was His Son.

> That which was from the beginning, which we have heard, which we have seen with our eyes, which we have looked upon, and our hands have handled, of the Word of life; (for the life was manifested, and we have seen it, and bear witness, and shew unto you that eternal life, which was with the Father, and was manifested unto us;) that which we have seen and heard declare we unto you, that ye also may have fellowship with us: and truly our fellowship is with the Father, and with his Son Jesus Christ. And these things write we unto you, that your joy may be full. (1 John 1:1–4)

> And after six days Jesus taketh Peter, James, and John his brother, and bringeth them up into an high mountain apart, and was transfigured before them: and his face did shine as the sun, and his raiment was white as the light. And, behold, there appeared unto them Moses and Elias talking with him. Then answered Peter, and said unto Jesus, Lord, it is good for us to be here: if thou wilt, let us make here three tabernacles; one for thee, and one for Moses, and one for Elias. While he yet spake, behold, a bright cloud overshadowed them: and behold a voice out of the cloud, which said, This is my beloved Son, in whom I am well pleased; hear ye him. (Matthew 17:1–5)

Peter, one of the three witnesses who had seen and heard the evidence that Christ was indeed the Son of God, explained that there was something yet more convincing than what he had seen and what he had heard. Peter unquestionably understood that our eyes and our ears can deceive us. Of course, we all understand this because magicians practice the art of deception before our eyes. One of the hallmarks of sports, for example, is that one player is seeking to deceive the other to gain an advantage. There is something far more certain than what we see and what we hear, or that which we receive from our neural receptors. We are referring to that certainty which comes from biblical prophecy. Here are the words of Peter. Ponder them carefully. Gather the full impact of what this Apostle is declaring:

> For we have not followed cunningly devised fables, when we made known unto you the power and coming of our Lord Jesus Christ, but were eyewitnesses of his majesty. For he received from God the Father honour and glory, when there came such a voice to him from the excellent glory, This is my beloved Son, in whom I am well pleased. And this voice which came from heaven we heard, when we were with him in the holy mount. We have also a more sure word of prophecy; whereunto ye do well that ye take heed, as unto a light that shineth in a dark place, until the day dawn, and the day star arise in your hearts: knowing this first, that no prophecy of the scripture is of any private interpretation. For the prophecy came not in old time by the will of man: but holy men of God spake as they were moved by the Holy Ghost. (2 Peter 1:16–21)

In this book, we will test the validity of prophecy as a revelation of an all-knowing God who indeed knows the end from the beginning; therefore, the future is as transparent to Him as the present or the past. It is through prophecy that we have an opportunity to test the validity of the Scriptures. It is through prophecy that we can establish the actual authenticity of the principles of human salvation. For, if prophecy is fulfilled with pinpoint accuracy, then surely we can trust the same God to lead men and women to Him and to His eternal kingdom. This concept is not only imbedded firmly in the Old Testament, it is just as surely imbedded in the New Testament. The students of prophecy have been given a great responsibility by God to share this evidence and share it with their fellow human beings.

> Bring forth the blind people that have eyes, and the deaf that have ears. . . . Ye are my witnesses, saith the Lord, and my servant whom I have chosen: that ye may know and believe me, and understand that I am he: before me there was no God formed, neither shall there be after me. . . . I have declared, and have saved, and I have shewed, when there was no strange god among you: therefore ye are my witnesses, saith the Lord, that I am God. (Isaiah 43:8–12)

The validity of God's sacred Scriptures, the Bible, is dependent upon the fulfillment of prophecy. God is determined that anyone who will seek to understand and genuinely desires to know whether there is an infinite, all-knowing God, will have all the evidence which he needs. In this book, we give some of the evidences of the existence of God by demonstrating the impossibility that many of these prophecies of the Bible could have been fulfilled at the time the prophets wrote them down or at any future time, claiming that these were the utterances which they received from God. It is the unwavering belief of the authors that no atheist, skeptic, nor agnostic, can stand against the mighty evidence of biblical prophecy.

CHAPTER 2
Sodom and Gomorrah

So let us begin our prophetic journey with the destiny of five of the most ancient cities known in past civilization—cities whose existence are well attested through archeological findings. The five cities of the plains had a well-earned reputation for wickedness. These cities, Sodom, Gomorrah, Admah, Zeboiim and Zoar, had turned to vile sexual practices. Sodom and Gomorrah are first referred to in Scripture in Genesis 10:19. They are identified as cities of the descendants of Ham, one of Noah's three sons. By the time Abram had settled in the land of Canaan, these cities were well established near the Dead Sea in what is in southern Israel today. Unlike today, the valley in which they were located was very fertile. It was for this reason that Lot, the nephew of Abram, selfishly chose the plain of Jordan, not far from Sodom, to take his flocks.

> And Lot lifted up his eyes, and beheld all the plain of Jordan, that it was well watered every where, before the Lord destroyed Sodom and Gomorrah, even as the garden of the Lord, like the land of Egypt, as thou comest unto Zoar. Then Lot chose him all the plain of Jordan; and Lot journeyed east: and they separated themselves the one from the other. Abram dwelled in the land of Canaan, and Lot dwelled in the cities of the plain, and pitched his tent toward Sodom. (Genesis 13:10–12)

However, the Bible exposes the vileness of the inhabitants of these cities. Apparently, at this time their evil practices were well known.

> But the men of Sodom were wicked and sinners before the LORD exceedingly. (Genesis 13:13)

It would appear that, soon thereafter, the five cities were attacked by four kings from the north.

> And it came to pass in the days of Amraphel king of Shinar, Arioch king of Ellasar, Chedorlaomer king of Elam, and Tidal king of nations; that these made war with Bera king of Sodom, and with Birsha king of Gomorrah, Shinab king of Admah, and Shemeber king of Zeboiim, and the king of Bela, which is Zoar. (Genesis 14:1–2)

In Genesis chapter 14 we read that for twelve years the five nations were subjected to King Chedorlaomer, king of Elam, after which they rebelled against their oppressor. However, the oppressor quickly suppressed the rebellion, and in the process Lot, the nephew of Abram, was taken captive. Upon hearing of this, Abram armed his servants, rescued Lot, and brought back all of the wealth and people who had been taken captive. While the king of Sodom was grateful for what Abram had done, sadly it did not lead to repentance of the Sodomites nor to an acceptance of the true God.

> And the king of Sodom said unto Abram, Give me the persons, and take the goods to thyself. And Abram said to the king of Sodom, I have lift up mine hand unto the LORD, the most high God, the possessor of heaven and earth, that I will not take from a thread even to a shoelatchet, and that I will not take any thing that is thine, lest thou shouldest say, I have made Abram rich. (Genesis 14:21–23)

Sadly, the wicked ways of Sodom and her sister cities continued.

One of the most amazing stories in the Bible which shows the great forbearance of God is associated with these base cities. Abram received a visit from the Lord and two angels appearing as men. After offering hospitality to them, Abram walked with them a little way toward Sodom. The Lord then confided to this man of God that these cities would be destroyed because of their fearful wickedness. Abram thought of his nephew and family, for now Lot no longer lived in the countryside close to Sodom; he was living in this wicked city itself. Abram was convinced that there must be righteous people even in this city. He dared to ask the Lord to spare the whole city if there were only fifty just men in the city. With holy boldness he pled with the Lord:

> And Abraham drew near, and said, Wilt thou also destroy the righteous with the wicked? Peradventure there be fifty righteous within the city: wilt thou also destroy and not spare the place for the fifty righteous that are therein? That be far from thee to do after this manner, to slay the righteous with the wicked: and that the righteous should be as the wicked, that be far from thee: Shall not the Judge of all the earth do right? (Genesis 18:23–25)

The Lord listened to the plea of his faithful servant and agreed to honor his request.

> And the LORD said, If I find in Sodom fifty righteous within the city, then I will spare all the place for their sakes. (Genesis 18:26)

However, even Abram must have doubted if there were fifty righteous men in Sodom, for successively he asked the Lord to spare Sodom for forty-five, forty, thirty, twenty and finally ten just men.

> Peradventure there shall lack five of the fifty righteous: wilt thou destroy all the city for lack of five? And he said, If I find there forty and five, I will not destroy it. And he spake unto him yet again, and said, Peradventure there shall be forty found there. And he said, I will not do it for forty's sake. And he said unto him, Oh let not the

> Lord be angry, and I will speak: Peradventure there shall thirty be found there. And he said, I will not do it, if I find thirty there. And he said, Behold now, I have taken upon me to speak unto the Lord: Peradventure there shall be twenty found there. And he said, I will not destroy it for twenty's sake. And he said, Oh let not the Lord be angry, and I will speak yet but this once: Peradventure ten shall be found there. And he said, I will not destroy it for ten's sake. (Genesis 18:28–32)

The Lord agreed, but not even ten inhabitants of this wicked city were righteous.

That same night, the wickedness of the Sodomites was revealed when the two angels lodged with Lot.

> But before they lay down, the men of the city, even the men of Sodom, compassed the house round, both old and young, all the people from every quarter: and they called unto Lot, and said unto him, Where are the men which came in to thee this night? bring them out unto us, that we may know them. (Genesis 19:4–5)

The cup of Sodom's iniquity had overflowed. Before the destruction of this diabolical city, the angels took Lot, his wife, and two daughters out of the city. Then they ordered fire and brimstone to rain upon the cities of the plains. In the end only three persons were saved, Lot and his two daughters, for Lot's wife disobeyed the command not to look back to Sodom and lost her life:

> But his wife looked back from behind him, and she became a pillar of salt. (Genesis 19:26)

Even to this day, the debauchery of Sodom is evident in the use of its name to designate homosexuals as sodomites, as was also the case in biblical times.

> And there were also sodomites in the land: and they did according to all the abominations of the nations which the Lord cast out before the children of Israel. (1 Kings 14:24)

So wicked were Sodom and Gomorrah that God declared three times that they would never be rebuilt.

> And Babylon, the glory of kingdoms, the beauty of the Chaldees' excellency, shall be as when God overthrew Sodom and Gomorrah. It shall never be inhabited, neither shall it be dwelt in from generation to generation: neither shall the Arabian pitch tent there; neither shall the shepherds make their fold there. (Isaiah 13:19–20)

> As in the overthrow of Sodom and Gomorrah and the neighbour cities thereof, saith the Lord, no man shall abide there, neither shall a son of man dwell in it. (Jeremiah 49:18)

> As God overthrew Sodom and Gomorrah and the neighbour cities thereof, saith the Lord; so shall no man abide there, neither shall any son of man dwell therein. (Jeremiah 50:40)

This is the most amazing prophecy against any ancient cities. Their destruction took place about 3,900 years ago. What an opportunity to prove the Word of God wrong! Building even one of these cities would accomplish this. Man has had nearly four millennia to rebuild these wicked cities. However, they cannot be rebuilt because the all-knowing God has decreed that they will not be rebuilt. Man is impotent to defy the prophecies of the Bible. This is definitive evidence that we can trust the Bible in matters of our eternal salvation.

Chapter 3
Nineveh, the Doomed City

NINEVEH was one of the earlier and famous of the cities of civilization. The Bible confirms that this city was built by Nimrod in the period of time soon after the world-wide flood, which had occurred during the lifetime of the biblical patriarch, Noah.

> And Cush begat Nimrod: he began to be a mighty one in the earth. He was a mighty hunter before the LORD: wherefore it is said, Even as Nimrod the mighty hunter before the LORD. And the beginning of his kingdom was Babel, and Erech, and Accad, and Calneh, in the land of Shinar. Out of that land went forth Asshur, and builded Nineveh, and the city Rehoboth, and Calah, and Resen between Nineveh and Calah: the same is a great city. (Genesis 10:8–12)

This would place its building in the late third millennium B.C. It flourished by the north bank of the Tigris River and had an abundant food supply from the rich valley between the Tigris and the Euphrates rivers. It eventually became the capital of the mighty Assyrian kingdom often spoken of in biblical history. There were times when no kingdom could stand against it—not even Babylon nor Egypt. It had a succession of kings who knew no defeat.

The Assyrian kingdom proper is thought to have arisen about 1900 B.C. From the Bible record, Nineveh was established some time before this by the great-grandson of Noah, Nimrod. The Bible record describes Nimrod as "a mighty hunter." Some believe that this means that he was a mighty warrior or war-lord. Scripture records that in his earlier life, he established four cities in the delta area of the Persian Gulf, often called the land of Shinar. The land of Shinar is without doubt what was later known as the land of Babylon and other nations such as the Chaldees.

> He was a mighty hunter before the LORD: wherefore it is said, Even as Nimrod the mighty hunter before the LORD. And the beginning of his kingdom was Babel, and Erech, and Accad, and Calneh, in the land of Shinar. (Genesis 10:9–10)

> And it shall come to pass in that day, that the Lord shall set his hand again the second time to recover the remnant of his people, which shall be left, from Assyria, and from Egypt, and from Pathros, and from Cush, and from Elam, and from Shinar, and from Hamath, and from the islands of the sea. (Isaiah 11:11)

> In the third year of the reign of Jehoiakim king of Judah came Nebuchadnezzar king of Babylon unto Jerusalem, and besieged it. And the Lord gave Jehoiakim king of Judah into his hand, with part of the vessels of the house of God: which he carried into the land of Shinar to the house of his god; and he brought the vessels into the treasure house of his god. (Daniel 1:1–2)

In these texts the prophets Isaiah and Daniel use the name Shinar as synonymous with Babylon.

These were cities which were later incorporated into the southeastern kingdom of Babylonia, which was headquartered in one of these four cities—Babel—later known as Babylon. Apparently not content with this notable achievement of building four cities, the Bible states that Nimrod left this region and established four more cities.

> Out of that land went forth Asshur, and builded Nineveh, and the city Rehoboth, and Calah, and Resen

between Nineveh and Calah: the same is a great city. (Genesis 10:11–12)

It would appear that the phrase "went forth Asshur" near the beginning of verse 11 in the King James Bible was not as good a translation as it could have been. A better rendition of the Hebrew would be the marginal reading, "he went out into Assyria." This verifies that Nimrod's journey was northwest, up the Tigris River, where he founded these four more new cities, Nineveh, Rehoboth, Calah, and Resen. The fact that the Genesis record calls the region the land of Assyria is not final proof that that name was well established at that time of Nimrod's building of these cities. Remember that Moses wrote this record in Genesis well over 500 years after Nimrod built the cities, a time when Assyria was well known.

It seems that Nineveh was not built up to any great extent by the succession of kings ruling Assyria. For many years during the second millennium B.C, Assyria was a rather weak nation, much inferior in power to the Hittite, Kassite, and Mitannian dynasties. It was not until the neo-Assyrian period that the city expanded under the rule of Ashurnasirpal II. However, it was left to Sennacherib to build Nineveh to be the magnificent city it became at the end of the eighth century and the beginning of the seventh century B.C.

Sennacherib, however, lost great prestige with his subjects when his army of 185,000 soldiers was slain by the angel of the Lord when he sought to conquer Jerusalem in the days of Isaiah the prophet and King Hezekiah.

> Then the angel of the LORD went forth, and smote in the camp of the Assyrians a hundred and fourscore and five thousand: and when they arose early in the morning, behold, they were all dead corpses. So Sennacherib king of Assyria departed, and went and returned, and dwelt at Nineveh. (Isaiah 37:36–37)

Upon learning that Sennacherib had been defeated, the Babylonians saw this as an opportune time to seek to free themselves from their subjection to the Assyrian king. However, somehow Sennacherib raised another powerful army and ruthlessly crushed the Babylonians, destroying the city and many of their temples and idols. Rather than being reinstated as a conquering hero when he returned to Assyria, he was even more hated, for some of the idols he had destroyed in Babylon were also worshipped by the Assyrians. Eventually, he was assassinated by two of his sons as the prophet Isaiah and the records of history attest.

> So Sennacherib king of Assyria departed, and went and returned, and dwelt at Nineveh. And it came to pass, as he was worshipping in the house of Nisroch his god, that Adrammelech and Sharezer his sons smote him with the sword; and they escaped into the land of Armenia: and Esarhaddon his son reigned in his stead. (Isaiah 37:37–38)

Well before the city of Babylon was built in all its beauty, Nineveh had been one of the most beautiful cities of the world. Years after the assassination of Sennacherib, Nineveh was brutally destroyed in 612 B.C. by the Chaldean king of Babylon, Nabopolassar, the father of Nebuchadnezzar, supported by the army of Cyaxares, the king of the Medes. He had sought revenge for Sennacherib's rape of Babylon. His overthrow of Nineveh doomed the Assyrian Empire, which never again rose to prominence and eventually vanished from the nations of the world.

What is so startling about this is the fact that Assyria was not another small tribal kingdom. It rose to great power in the world. It had conquered the kingdom of Israel and taken people captive. It had defeated Egypt, Syria, and Babylon at its height. There seemed no power of antiquity which could offer a serious challenge to Assyria's might.

God had done everything to save Nineveh from her wickedness. In compassion He sent the reluctant messenger, Jonah, to warn her people to repent of their wickedness. For a time, they repented and God spared them. (See the chapter entitled "Unfulfilled Prophecies.")

> And God saw their works, that they turned from their evil way; and God repented of the evil, that he had said

that he would do unto them; and he did it not. (Jonah 3:10)

However, clearly the Ninevites turned back to their old ways. God in His long patience sent a message from another prophet—Nahum, who predicted its total destruction while it was still a powerful nation. Nahum refers to the terrible results of their wickedness.

> And it shall come to pass, that all they that look upon thee shall flee from thee, and say, Nineveh is laid waste: who will bemoan her? whence shall I seek comforters for thee? (Nahum 3:7)

Note how complete this prophecy was fulfilled.

> In the following year 612, both the Chaldeans and the Medes besieged Nineveh which they took in the month of Ab (August) of that year. The city was looted and completely destroyed *never to be rebuilt again.* (*Encyclopedia Britannica*, 1968 edition, volume 2, 967)

Some may claim that other great cities have vanished forever. Other than where God has prophesized such, we know of no other great ancient city as prominent as was Nineveh which is not existing today. For example, at the time of the destruction of Nineveh the cities of Alexandria (Egypt); Damascus (Syria) and Jerusalem (Judah) were in existence, and today they are still notable cities. The cities God said would be destroyed have been laid waste and none has been re-established. God's book of infinite wisdom again stands the test of investigation. While God is a longsuffering God, there is a limit to His patience with nations and people. These biblical records are sobering reminders to those of us living close to the end of this wicked world's history. Why in twenty-six centuries has Nineveh not been rebuilt? God knew that never again would it be rebuilt. The present city of Mosul, Iraq is located not far from ancient Nineveh; however, it is not located on the north side of the Tigris river, but on the south side.

Just as nations have their time of probation, so do members of the human race. The understanding of these prophecies and their fulfillment give warning of our need to be surrendered fully to the power of Christ and His wonderful grace which, if received, will lead us to eternal salvation.

CHAPTER 4
A King's Dream

WHEN the authors were lads, every year we would accompany our parents to evangelistic crusades conducted by men who earnestly unfolded many fascinating prophecies from the Bible. Almost as far back as we can remember, we heard one of the most intriguing prophecies which has been fulfilled in history. So startling is this prophecy that many skeptics and critics of the Bible have claimed that it was not written in the sixth century B.C., when it was decoded and recorded by a young Jewish captive named Daniel. This prophecy has unfolded with such amazing accuracy that these skeptics have tried to place its origin much later than when it was written in an effort to "prove" that it was not a miraculous prophecy from God, but rather was the telling of events which had already transpired. At the end of this chapter, we will explain why this entire attempt to discredit the interpretation of this dream proves to be without merit, for the dream does not stop at the second century B.C. (when some claim that it was written). Rather, its fulfillment reaches into the Christian era, and ultimately, to a prophecy concerning the return of Jesus. Let us look at this prophecy found in the second chapter of the Old Testament book of Daniel.

Who was Daniel? The events surrounding Daniel are very well known in history. The history of this period is found in many books which detail ancient history. Added to the events described by Daniel is history's record of the Chaldean king of Babylon, Nabopolassar, who, with the help of Cyaxares, king of the Medes (*Encyclopaedia Britannica*, 1993, vol. 8, p. 171), had gained great power and succeeded in utterly destroying Nineveh, the capital of the Assyrian kingdom, a kingdom under which the Babylonians had been subjected. (See chapter entitled, "Nineveh, the Doomed City.") Nabopolassar had a son who was destined to be his successor and who was to achieve much greater fame than his father. His son, Nebuchadnezzar, who reigned for 44 years (Ibid.), was given the responsibility of expanding the Babylonian Empire. He proved to be a mighty military leader.

Nebuchadnezzar led a great army from Babylon across what was called the Fertile Crescent, along the valley between the Euphrates and Tigris Rivers, down to where the Babylonians conquered Syria. Then, traveling further south from Syria in 605 B.C., he defeated the Egyptians and subdued the Jews in the same year. He took some of the finest Jewish artisans and wisest young princes of Judah captive. The artisans were engaged in the massive building program which made Babylon the most magnificent city of antiquity. The young princes were chosen to be educated in the ways of the Babylonians and to assume leadership roles in the government of the Babylonian kingdom. These captives included four young princes by name—Daniel, Hananiah, Mishael, and Azariah. Although there were many other Jews taken captive, yet only these four remained faithful and unwavering to the principles and faith which they had learned as boys growing up in Judah. (See Daniel 1:8–19)

While on this military campaign, Nebuchadnezzar received the startling news that his father, Nabopolassar had died. Seeking quickly to secure the kingdom before other pretenders or usurpers might take it over, Nebuchadnezzar and a few loyal and trusted aids, in one of the epic journeys of history, traveled diagonally across the desert, and it is said that within ten days he had arrived at Babylon to take up the scepter of rulership. On the other hand, the prisoners, carefully chosen from the Jewish artisans and from the elite class of Judah, were taken and chained together for the long journey north up to the Tigris and Euphrates valley, and then southeast to Babylon. History indicates that this journey took about four months.

Much of the book of Daniel is written in the first person; therefore, the author of most of the book claims to be Daniel himself. What gives great credibility to this claim is the fact that Daniel gives so much detail about the events which took place. In the first chapter, we learn of some of Nebuchadnezzar's most trusted officials. For example, in Daniel 1:3, we learn that the master of the eunuchs was Ashpenaz. We learn that Ashpenaz gave those captives Babylonian names. Daniel's Babylonian name was Belteshazzar. Hananiah was given the name of Shadrach, Mishael the name Meshach, and Azariah became Abednego (See Daniel 1:3–6). There is no question that these were not Jewish names, rather they were Babylonian. Indeed, Daniel's new name, Belteshazzar, tied him to the god Bel, one of the "great" god's of Babylon.

We also learn in the first chapter of the book of Daniel that Ashpenaz had an assistant, Melzar, who was put in charge over Daniel, Hananiah, Azariah, and Mishael. While the Bible does not specifically state that the Jewish captives were castrated and thus made eunuchs, nevertheless, we know that this was a common practice of the Babylonians with those whom they decided to train as leaders from the nations they conquered. The fact that they were put in charge under the prince of the eunuchs (see Daniel 1:7, 9–10) clearly confirms that these young princes went through this sad experience.

Nebuchadnezzar was ultimately to make two more invasions of Judah. In response to the rebellion of the Jewish kings, these invasions almost certainly would not have taken place if these kings had remained vassals, paying tribute and serving under the Babylonian king. In the last of these invasions, the magnificent temple of Solomon was utterly destroyed, and huge numbers of Jews were taken and placed in servitude, doing much of the work in the completion of the building of the great city of Babylon which some claim was the grandest city ever built. However, the wise young princes of Judah were given various supervisory responsibilities.

In Daniel 1:10, we learn that the four Jewish princes were given the highest honor of sitting at the king's table and that they could partake of the meat and drink which was apportioned to the king himself. However, these Jewish young men realized that the food which was offered to idols and the alcoholic wine was not consistent with the principles in which they had been trained as boys. Therefore, they explained to Melzar, their immediate supervisor, saying that they would not eat or drink of the king's portion. This was an extraordinarily dangerous decision, but God honored these young men. Melzar was very nervous about conceding to their request, believing that they would be weak and that they would not be able to measure up to the requirements which the king had in the wisdom and learning of Babylon and for which they were in training. They asked Melzar to test them for ten days.

> Prove thy servants, I beseech thee, ten days; and let them give us pulse to eat, and water to drink. . . . So he consented to them in this matter, and proved them ten days. (Daniel 1:12, 14)

Reluctantly, Melzar agreed to prove them. The Bible assures us that they proved to be by far the wisest of all the trainees. No doubt, God entrusted them with great wisdom so that they could prove that the simple diet they chose was conducive to health and wisdom. In the end, king Nebuchadnezzar began to take note of these young men. The biblical record says,

> And the king communed with them; and among them all was found none like Daniel, Hananiah, Mishael, and Azariah: therefore stood they before the king. And in all matters of wisdom and understanding, that the king enquired of them, he found them ten times better than all the magicians and astrologers that were in all his realm. (Daniel 1:19–20)

However, a crisis arose. One night, Nebuchadnezzar had a dream. Clearly this dream had made a deep impression upon him; yet, as he awakened in the morning, try as he might, he could not remember the details of the dream. As was the custom in this pagan nation, immediately the king called the men who were thought to be wise in the understanding of dreams.

> Then the king commanded to call the magicians, and the astrologers, and the sorcerers, and the Chaldeans, for

> to shew the king his dreams. So they came and stood
> before the king. (Daniel 2:2)

No doubt in times past these "wise" men had given the interpretation of Nebuchadnezzar's dreams, but here was a difficult and altogether more complicated situation. On this occasion the king could not remember the dream, so he confronted these men by demanding that they tell him what he had dreamed. It was not difficult for these men to manufacture interpretations of dreams which the king had recited to them, but now they were faced with the dilemma of not even knowing what the dream was. As hard as they tried, they could not tell the king the dream. Nebuchadnezzar had zero tolerance for the inability of these men to bring to his attention the details of his dream.

> For this cause the king was angry and very furious,
> and commanded to destroy all the wise men of Babylon.
> And the decree went forth that the wise men should be
> slain; and they sought Daniel and his fellows to be slain.
> (Daniel 2:12–13)

The decree not only affected the men who had stood before the king, but also the young trainees in wisdom—Daniel, Hananiah, Mishael, and Azariah. In rounding up the wise men, Arioch, the captain of the king's guard, came to take these four men, to slay them along with the others. In a calm, but firm voice, Daniel challenged Arioch.

> He answered and said to Arioch the king's captain,
> Why is the decree so hasty from the king? Then Arioch
> made the thing known to Daniel. (Daniel 2:15)

After requesting time from the king, Daniel and his friends earnestly prayed that the God of heaven would reveal to them the king's dream.

> Then Daniel went in, and desired of the king that he
> would give him time, and that he would shew the king the

> interpretation. Then Daniel went to his house, and made the thing known to Hananiah, Mishael, and Azariah, his companions: that they would desire mercies of the God of heaven concerning this secret; that Daniel and his fellows should not perish with the rest of the wise men of Babylon. Then was the secret revealed unto Daniel in a night vision. Then Daniel blessed the God of heaven. Daniel answered and said, Blessed be the name of God for ever and ever: for wisdom and might are his: and he changeth the times and the seasons: he removeth kings, and setteth up kings: he giveth wisdom unto the wise, and knowledge to them that know understanding: he revealeth the deep and secret things: he knoweth what is in the darkness, and the light dwelleth with him. I thank thee, and praise thee, O thou God of my fathers, who hast given me wisdom and might, and hast made known unto me now what we desired of thee: for thou hast now made known unto us the king's matter. (Daniel 2:16–23)

In a great act of mercy and compassion toward the deceptive magicians and astrologers, Daniel pled for their lives.

> Therefore Daniel went in unto Arioch, whom the king had ordained to destroy the wise men of Babylon: he went and said thus unto him; Destroy not the wise men of Babylon: bring me in before the king, and I will shew unto the king the interpretation. (Daniel 2:24)

The Bible record attests that Arioch, seeking no doubt the favor of the king, seized the opportunity to introduce Daniel to Nebuchadnezzar.

> Then Arioch brought in Daniel before the king in haste, and said thus unto him, I have found a man of the captives of Judah, that will make known unto the king the interpretation. (Daniel 2:25)

When taken before the king, Daniel first pointed out the futility of relying upon the pagan wise men, the astrologers, the magicians and the soothsayers. Yet, instead of boasting about what he could do, he gave all the glory to God, making it plain to this pagan king that what he was to present was not his own wisdom but had come directly from the Creator God of the universe.

> Daniel answered in the presence of the king, and said, The secret which the king hath demanded cannot the wise men, the astrologers, the magicians, the soothsayers, shew unto the king; but there is a God in heaven that revealeth secrets, and maketh known to the king Nebuchadnezzar what shall be in the latter days. Thy dream, and the visions of thy head upon thy bed, are these. (Daniel 2:27–28)

Then immediately he explained the dream which the king had forgotten. It was a simple dream, and immediately it came back to the king's memory as it was unfolded by Daniel.

> Thou, O king, sawest, and behold a great image. This great image, whose brightness was excellent, stood before thee; and the form thereof was terrible. This image's head was of fine gold, his breast and his arms of silver, his belly and his thighs of brass, his legs of iron, his feet part of iron and part of clay. Thou sawest till that a stone was cut out without hands, which smote the image upon his feet that were of iron and clay, and brake them to pieces. Then was the iron, the clay, the brass, the silver, and the gold, broken to pieces together, and became like the chaff of the summer threshingfloors; and the wind carried them away, that no place was found for them: and the stone that smote the image became a great mountain, and filled the whole earth. (Daniel 2:31–35)

Nebuchadnezzar was amazed, for indeed this was exactly the dream which he had dreamed. Now he could trust this young prophet of God to explain the dream.

However, the dream could not have been pleasing to Nebuchadnezzar. Like all successful leaders, he had in his mind that he would set up a kingdom which would never be destroyed, but the dream indicated otherwise. Here are the words of the prophet as he explained the meaning of the dream to King Nebuchadnezzar. Now keep in mind that this prophecy was expounded more than twenty-five hundred years ago; however, it dealt with plain detail which can easily be checked by any infidel, agnostic, skeptic, or atheist.

> . . . Thou art this head of gold. And after thee shall arise another kingdom inferior to thee, and another third kingdom of brass, which shall bear rule over all the earth. And the fourth kingdom shall be strong as iron: forasmuch as iron breaketh in pieces and subdueth all things: and as iron that breaketh all these, shall it break in pieces and bruise. And whereas thou sawest the feet and toes, part of potters' clay, and part of iron, the kingdom shall be divided; but there shall be in it of the strength of the iron, forasmuch as thou sawest the iron mixed with miry clay. And as the toes of the feet were part of iron, and part of clay, so the kingdom shall be partly strong, and partly broken. And whereas thou sawest iron mixed with miry clay, they shall mingle themselves with the seed of men: but they shall not cleave one to another, even as iron is not mixed with clay. And in the days of these kings shall the God of heaven set up a kingdom, which shall never be destroyed: and the kingdom shall not be left to other people, but it shall break in pieces and consume all these kingdoms, and it shall stand for ever. (Daniel 2:38–44)

It will be noted that four kingdoms are identified. The first kingdom, represented by this head of gold as verse 38 explains, refers to Babylon, of which Nebuchadnezzar was king. In the plainest of words Daniel said, "Thou art this head of gold." Notice that in verse 39 it does not say that "after thee shall arise another *king*." That would be expected.

Instead, it said "after thee shall arise another *kingdom* inferior." Indeed, Babylon was followed by the kingdom of Medo-Persia, represented by the silver. This kingdom would then be followed by a third kingdom represented by the brass and finally a fourth kingdom which was represented by iron. Yet, no such all-encompassing kingdom was to follow this fourth kingdom. History is very clear so that we cannot fail in the identification of the three succeeding kingdoms after Babylon. It was the Medo-Persians who conquered Babylon, not in the lifetime of Nebuchadnezzar but during the reign of his grandson, Belshazzar, in 539 B.C.

Eventually, the power of the Medo-Persian Empire gave way in 324 B.C. to the even mightier power of the Macedonian King Alexander of Greece. Greece became an even greater conquering power than was either Babylon or Medo-Persia before it. Yet, it too was later to succumb in 161 B.C., this time to the iron rule of Rome, which was not only to become the most powerful of the four kingdoms, but also the nation which spread its empire much further than the other three kingdoms and ruled many centuries longer, until the end of the fifth century (476 A.D.).

Amazingly in line with the prophecy, no other single conquering nation arose after Rome. Rather, as the decadent Western Roman Empire collapsed, it divided into ten separate kingdoms, exactly as the toes of the image indicate. As confirmed by Gibbon in his definitive work entitled *The Decline and Fall of the Roman Empire*, these kingdoms were well defined. They were as follows: Alamanni, Ostrogoths, Visigoths, Franks, Vandals, Suevi, Burgundians, Heruli, Anglo-Saxons, and the Lombards.

The prophecy does not directly draw attention to the number of the toes, however we will see in another of Daniel's prophecy (in chapter 7), that the number ten is very significantly detailed in its expansion upon the facts of this prophecy. However, this prophecy alone is amazing. The division of the Roman Empire is such that it has never been restored throughout the subsequent history of Europe. Some turn to the development of the European Union and suggest that Europe will eventually become one single United States of Europe. But, this prophecy is plain that this will not be fully achieved.

> And whereas thou sawest iron mixed with miry clay, they shall mingle themselves with the seed of men: but they shall not cleave one to another, even as iron is not mixed with clay. (Daniel 2:43)

The prophecy details that the nations will mingle one with the other, but they will not cleave together. In other words, they will not become one nation. When we review the efforts to bring about a united Europe, we are amazed at the accuracy of this prophecy which has endured the test of history.

The first desire to unite all of Europe was attempted by Charlemagne. He was a very successful conqueror, but in his reign from 800–814, he did not come close to ruling all of Europe. There have been others with expansionist goals—Napoleon of France, Kaiser Wilhelm and Adolph Hitler of Germany. Yet, while each one of those expansionists had dramatic successes, in the end they failed, for God's Word cannot fail.

Queen Victoria had a great desire to unite the monarchs of Europe by the intermarriage of all the European monarchies. Though she succeeded to a great extent in matchmaking the princes of Europe with the princesses, nevertheless, it indeed did not bring peace or unity. It is educative to see that first cousins Czar Nicolas II of Russia, Kaiser Wilhelm II of Germany, and King George V of Great Britain found themselves fighting against each other in World War I. All those were the grandsons of Queen Victoria. What a simple but amazing prophecy! Of course, Nebuchadnezzar did not live to see even the demise of his own nation, but with unwavering accuracy, these events have come to pass.

What would have been the probability of a fallible human being concocting this prophecy and having it all come true? Who could have predicted that no European nation would follow the Roman Empire? Who would have predicted that it would break up into exactly ten kingdoms? Who would have predicted that the nations of Europe would not rejoin into one great nation? We can be just as confident that the sovereignty of European nations will not be totally destroyed by the European Union because the Word of the Lord has spoken. We can trust Holy Scripture.

CHAPTER 5
Four Beasts, Ten Horns, and a Little Horn

WELL after the death of Nebuchadnezzar, when his grandson Belshazzar was reigning, Daniel had a dream. Although this dream, in its basic imagery, was quite different from the dream of Nebuchadnezzar, yet it proved to be a dream which was repeating and expanding upon the dream of Nebuchadnezzar. God was making sure that we would be in no doubt as to the fulfillment of these prophecies.

Daniel 7 depicts four animals, the first being a lion with eagle's wings (verse 4). This is followed by a bear which is raised up on one side and has three ribs in its mouth (verse 5). The third beast is a leopard which had four wings of a fowl and four heads (verse 6). Finally, there is a beast which Daniel could not identify except that it was

> . . . dreadful and terrible, and strong exceedingly; and it had great iron teeth: it devoured and brake in pieces, and stamped the residue with the feet of it: and it was diverse from all the beasts that were before it; and it had ten horns. (Verse 7)

Just as there were four metals described in Daniel 2, now there were four beasts. We do not have to guess who the first beast represents, for Babylon was famous for its depictions of the winged lion, symbolizing the power, might, and speed with which it would overrun and conquer other nations. Today in the Brandenburg museum in Berlin can be seen some of the remnants of the walls and buildings of ancient Babylon, and amongst them are seen depictions of the lion with wings. There is no question that Daniel would have understood very clearly that this first beast represented Babylon.

So that we would not have any difficulty about the next kingdom as representing Medo-Persia, it is well defined as a bear being raised up on one side. This showed the superiority of one of the two united nations which had overthrown Babylon. While in the early days the Medes were the more powerful, very quickly Persia became the dominant partner in the Medo-Persian Empire. What, however, are the three ribs in the mouth of the bear? These represented the three powers which would be overcome by Medo-Persia—Lydia, Babylon, and Egypt. (For those who may not be familiar with the territory once occupied by Lydia, that kingdom was within the region of Western Turkey today.) We are always amazed at how accurate the Bible prophecies are. There were not four ribs, nor were there two, but there were the exact number of the nations which the Medo-Persian armies subjugated.

The third beast is described as a leopard having four wings of a fowl and four heads. The rapidity of the conquests of Alexander the Great was such that undoubtedly these four wings were representative of the speed with which Alexander conquered all the way to India, the Middle East, North Africa, and in some areas of Europe.

Now, what about the four heads? We now have the perspective of history. In tragic circumstances, still in his early thirties, Alexander drank himself to death when mourning the death of one of his closest friends. This threw the Greek Empire into chaos. The generals of Alexander along with other claimants to the throne fought for the right to be the next ruler. However, just as surely as the Bible said there would be four heads or four powers, so that became the reality. Eventually only four generals were left. For a period of twelve years, there were desperate internal struggles during which various regions of the empire changed hands, often a number of times. Two of the claimants as kings were killed until only Antigonus I emerged as the last pretender to the rulership of the whole empire. However, the four generals formed a coalition against Antigonus and fought against him. Antigonus was killed, his son Demetrius fled, and the four generals set themselves up as kings in the divided regions of the empire. Ptolemy ruled Egypt, Palestine, and part of Syria—the southern part of the Greek Empire. Cassander ruled Macedonia and to some extent Greece, becoming king of the west. Lysimachus ruled Thrace and a large part of Asia Minor and became king of the north. Seleucus became king of the East, including the bulk of what had been the Persian Empire, parts of Asia Minor, northern Syria, Mesopotamia, and the East. Once again the exactitude of biblical prophecy was fulfilled.

Thus weakened by this division in 301 B.C., the power of the Grecian kingdom gradually began to erode. By 200 B.C., Rome became the controller of the western Mediterranean area. In 197 B.C., Rome defeated Macedonia. In 190 B.C., Rome defeated Antiochus III and took the Seleucid territory. In 168 B.C., Rome ended the monarchy of Macedonia and now had effectively become the powerhouse succeeding the rulership of Grecian Empire.

By the time of the birth of Christ, Rome was unchallengeably the greatest power on the face of the planet. It had extended its territory all the way to the British Isles. It was dominating northern Africa, the Middle East, and territories beyond. In verse 8 of Daniel 7, as the prophet was considering the ten horns, he witnessed a little horn coming up, which plucked up three of the ten horns. In the previous chapter, "A King's Dream," we identified the ten toes as the ten kingdoms which were established after the fall of the Roman Empire. Here they are again depicted, this time as horns. In Daniel 2, there was no reference, however, to the three kingdoms which were "plucked up."

History has not left us in doubt as to the three kingdoms which disappeared. Each one had opposed the establishment of the powerful religio-political power known as the papacy which had arisen to great power in the first part of the sixth century. At this time, these three of the ten powers of Europe were branded by Rome as holding Arian views. The Arians were said to believe that the Father alone is God (therefore, He alone is eternal, wise, good, and unchangeable), and the Son of God is preexistent of all other creatures, but He is not eternal. These nations which were thus stigmatized as "Arians" were the Ostrogoths, the Heruli, and the Vandals. Amazingly, and without clear historical understanding, they disappeared. Here we draw the attention of the readers again to what history records:

They [the Heruli] raided towns in the Roman Empire, scoring their greatest success in A.D. 267, when they captured Byzantium and sacked Greek cities. Two years later, the eastern Heruli were crushingly defeated by the Roman emperor Claudius II Gothicus in a battle near Naissus (modern Niš, Yugos.). From then until the mid-6th century, when they vanished from history, their fortunes varied. ("Heruli," *Encyclopaedia Britannica 2007 Ultimate Reference Suite.*)

In one campaigning season [533–534] the Vandal kingdom was destroyed. Rome again ruled the area and restored the churches to the Roman Catholics. The Vandals played no further role in history. ("Vandal." Ibid.)

Theodoric became king of Italy in 493 and died in 526. A period of instability then ensued in the ruling dynasty, provoking the Byzantine emperor Justinian to declare war on the Ostrogoths in 535 in an effort to wrest Italy from their grasp. The war continued with varying fortunes for almost 20 years and caused untold damage to Italy, and the Ostrogoths thereafter had no national existence. ("Ostrogoth." Ibid.)

With amazing accuracy, the Bible record is true. The three nations which were "plucked up by the roots"—the Heruli, Vandals, and Ostrogoths—were the most formidable rivals to the Roman Catholic Church. The Heruli were the first of these nations to rule over Rome, led by Odoacer in 476. The next invasion of Rome came from the Ostrogoths under Theodoric in 493. The warlike Vandals under Genseric were the next to challenge the Catholic Church in the west. However, Emperor Justinian, reigning in Constantinople, responded by sending his general Belisarius with a strong army, which completely vanquished the Vandals in 534 A.D. In 538 A.D., Justinian sent another army, and the Ostrogoths were driven from Rome. They reentered Rome in 540 A.D., but their efforts were short lived. Like the other two "Arian" nations, they disappeared from the face of history. Once again, what seemed like wholly improbable prophecies proved to be the foretelling of history in advance.

Now Let us return to this little horn power. This power is described as having

> . . . eyes like the eyes of man, and a mouth speaking great things. (Daniel 7:8)

This power is said to persecute fearfully the saints of God and to attempt to change the law of God. He was also to rule for a long period of time, which is discussed in the chapter entitled "The Papal Deadly Wound." Many Christian commentators rightly have identified this little horn power which was to become such a force in society as none other than the papacy of Rome.

> Out of the ruins of political Rome, arose the great moral Empire in the "giant form" of the Roman Church. (Alexander C. Flick, *The Rise of the Mediaeval Church*, 1909, p. 150)

Chapter 6

A Ram and a He Goat

STUDENTS of biblical prophecy have long recognized that the prophet Daniel received sequential visions and interpretations from God, each of which expand and add to the information which was revealed in previous prophecies regarding events yet future. This process is often called "repeat and enlarge." We have already examined the prophecy of Daniel 2, in which God not only revealed to Daniel the details of the dream which King Nebuchadnezzar had forgotten, but He also revealed the meaning of the future events which this prophecy foretold. Daniel was a very young man at this time, a captive Jew in training to be a leader in Nebuchadnezzar's kingdom. However, in Daniel's old age he had two dreams about two years apart.

We have already examined the dream which he received well after the death of Nebuchadnezzar, in the first year of the reign of Belshazzar. This dream and interpretation is recorded in Daniel 7. Our explanation of this chapter is recorded in the chapter entitled "Four Beasts, Ten Horns, and a Little Horn." That prophecy expanded upon the prophecy of Daniel 2.

In Daniel 8 we have the record of the vision in the third year of the reign of King Belshazzar. The dreams recorded in Daniel 7 and 8 respectively do not contradict any of the details of Daniel 2. Though they were received many decades later, both enlarge on the details given in Nebuchadnezzar's dream. Below are the introductory verses to the prophecy of Daniel 8.

> In the third year of the reign of king Belshazzar a vision appeared unto me, even unto me Daniel, after that which

appeared unto me at the first. And I saw in a vision; and it came to pass, when I saw, that I was at Shushan in the palace, which is in the province of Elam; and I saw in a vision, and I was by the river of Ulai. Then I lifted up mine eyes, and saw, and, behold, there stood before the river a ram which had two horns: and the two horns were high; but one was higher than the other, and the higher came up last. I saw the ram pushing westward, and northward, and southward; so that no beasts might stand before him, neither was there any that could deliver out of his hand; but he did according to his will, and became great. And as I was considering, behold, an he goat came from the west on the face of the whole earth, and touched not the ground: and the goat had a notable horn between his eyes. (Daniel 8:1–5)

Before investigating the symbolism of the ram and the he goat, let us explore the mystery of King Belshazzar. Skeptics and higher critical biblical scholars of the nineteenth century believed that the Bible miracles were fictitious or at the least allegorical. Thus because they believed that the details given in the book of Daniel did not predict the miraculous details of events yet to transpire, they charged that someone falsely claiming to be Daniel had written these events not in the sixth century B.C. but in the second century B.C., after the kingdom of Rome had become the dominant power of the planet. Thus the "fraudulent" claims of the author to be Daniel could be deciphered. It was claimed that instead of these prophecies being miraculous revelations of God, the author was actually recording previous history which had already transpired.

Part of their support for this assertion was the introduction in Daniel chapters 4, 7, and 8 of King Belshazzar, a king who had not been discovered in historical records until the middle of the nineteenth century. Thus the higher critics believed that Belshazzar was a fictitious name invented by the bogus author of the book of Daniel after the events transpired and was created to sound like a Babylonian name constructed around the name of the Babylonian god, Bel. Of course, that theory did not explain why these prophecies correctly explained that no other super-political militaristic power would develop after the overthrow of the Roman Empire and that never again would there be an individual superpower in the European-Asia Minor-North African sphere, even to this day.

Let us focus upon the historicity of King Belshazzar. Today, no credible Bible scholar or historian could deny his historicity. We have the most credible evidence that indeed there was a King Belshazzar who ruled at the time of the Medo-Persian conquest of Babylon and was killed at the time of that invasion.

In the last 150 years, the evidence of this king's existence is beyond valid questioning. Up to the middle of the nineteenth century, the historical evidence that was found consistently mentioned that the king who was ruling Babylon at the end of the Babylonian Empire was Nabonidus. Known history now confirms that Nabonidus became king of Babylon in 546 B.C. and that he was the father of Belshazzar. It is likely that Nabonidus was the son of a woman of Haran, maybe a wife or concubine of Nebuchadnezzar. As cuneiform texts have been discovered and translated, evidence of Belshazzar is abundant. It has been revealed that Belshazzar was coregent with his father Nabonidus. For many years, Nabonidus lived in Taima, Arabia, leaving the day-to-day kingship activities in Babylon to his son Belshazzar. In 1929 Raymond Dougherty of Yale University collected in one monograph all the available materials concerning the reign of Nabonidus and Belshazzar, titled *Nabonidus and Belshazzar* (New Haven: Yale, 1929, p. 216ff). The authenticating of the book of Daniel's record concerning Belshazzar was a deep blow to the skeptics and the scholars from the higher critical schools of theology.

Now we turn to the prophecy of Daniel 8. Who are represented by the ram and the he-goat? Daniel leaves us in no doubt. Daniel's information was provided by the senior angel from heaven—Gabriel:

> And I heard a man's voice between the banks of Ulai, which called, and said, Gabriel, make this man to understand the vision. (Daniel 8:16)

Gabriel gave an explanation of the vision, and the two beasts are clearly identified.

> The ram which thou sawest having two horns are the kings of Media and Persia. And the rough goat is the king of Grecia: and the great horn that is between his eyes is the first king. (Daniel 8:20–21)

Now these two great empires are clearly the same powers as are represented by the second and third segments of the image dreamed by Nebuchadnezzar—the silver breast and arms (Medo-Persia) and the belly and thighs of brass (Greece). It is very significant that, unlike Nebuchadnezzar's dream of chapter 2 and Daniel's dream in chapter 7, there is no mention of the kingdom of Babylon. This was no doubt because of the impending doom of Babylon, which soon would collapse under the withering assault of the mighty Medo-Persian army. This historical event took place in 539 B.C.

After the death of King Nebuchadnezzar in 562 B.C. there were two short reigns, Evil-Merodach (561 B.C. to 560 B.C.) and his brother-in-law, Neriglissar (559 B.C. to 556 B.C.). It was then that Nabonidus usurped the throne after the assassination of the heir Labashi-Marduk, a minor. This is the simple explanation of the *Encyclopedia Britannica* of the reign of Nabonidus:

> Internal difficulties and the recognition that the narrow strip of land from the Persian Gulf to Syria could not be defended against a major attack from the east induced Nabonidus to leave Babylonia around 552 and to reside in Taima (Taymā') in northern Arabia. There he organized an Arabian province with the assistance of Jewish mercenaries. His viceroy in Babylonia was his son Bel-shar-usur, the Belshazzar of the Book of Daniel in the Bible. ("Mesopotamia, history of." *Encyclopædia Britannica 2007 Ultimate Reference Suite*)

While Nebuchadnezzar is referred to in Daniel 5:2 as the father of Belshazzar, it is agreed by most authorities that Nebuchadnezzar was his grandfather. (See "Belshazzar." Ibid.) It was not uncommon for Jews to refer to an ancestor as their "father." Today we use the term "forefather."

> And think not to say within yourselves, We have Abraham to our father: for I say unto you, that God is able of these stones to raise up children unto Abraham. (Matthew 3:9)

Now to the vision. It is not clear whether Daniel was in Shushan bodily or simply in vision. What is significant is that Shushan became a Medo-Persian province, though it had been a Babylonian city previously. Maybe the location of Shushan and its Medo-Persian identification was a foreboding of the conquest of Babylon by the Medo-Persians.

There are some parallels between this prophecy of Daniel 2 and the prophecy of Daniel 7 in that the ram representing Medo-Persia was described as having 2 horns. This in itself is not unusual of a ram, but the prophecy identifies the fact that one horn was higher than the other. This parallels the bear-like beast of Daniel 7, which represented the Medo-Persian power, with one side raised higher than the other. Both descriptions were indicative that the Persians (now Iranians) would come to prominence after the Medes, and the Persians became the dominant partner when Cyrus, the king of the Persians, conquered Astyages, king of the Medes, in a battle that lasted from 553 to 550 B.C. However, with considerable wisdom, rather than placing the Medes in servitude, Cyrus accepted them as part of his confederacy, thus greatly empowering his kingdom, which was to be critical in the defeat of the Babylonians. Eventually this kingdom at its zenith was to extend from Egypt to India. The Bible described this empire as "great."

> I saw the ram pushing westward, and northward, and southward; so that no beasts might stand before him, neither was there any that could deliver out of his hand; but he did according to his will, and became great. (Daniel 8:4)

However there was to arise another mighty military power which would overcome the power of the Medo-Persian Empire. In 331 B.C., the youthful Alexander of Macedonia proved himself to be one of the most successful conquerors of all history, raising up the powerful Greek

Empire which conquered with fearsome military assaults. The Scripture is very descriptive.

> And as I was considering, behold, an he goat came from the west on the face of the whole earth, and touched not the ground: and the goat had a notable horn between his eyes. And he came to the ram that had two horns, which I had seen standing before the river, and ran unto him in the fury of his power. And I saw him come close unto the ram, and he was moved with choler against him, and smote the ram, and brake his two horns: and there was no power in the ram to stand before him, but he cast him down to the ground, and stamped upon him: and there was none that could deliver the ram out of his hand. (Daniel 8:5–7)

It will be noted that both the Medes and Persians were overthrown, represented by the breaking of the two horns of the ram.

We must not overlook the notable horn between the eyes of the he-goat. The angel Gabriel did not leave any doubt as to who was represented by the notable horn. So well known is the first king of the mighty Greek Empire that most older school children could identify him as Alexander the Great. His empire was described as "very great," thus greater than the Medo-Persian Empire.

> Therefore the he goat waxed very great: and when he was strong, the great horn was broken; and for it came up four notable ones toward the four winds of heaven. (Daniel 8:8)

Here is his identification.

> And the rough goat is the king of Grecia: and the great horn that is between his eyes is the first king. (Daniel 8:21)

Yet the first king of the Greek Empire, Alexander, was not to survive long. He died of a serious fever, most likely the consequence of alcoholic poisoning at age 32 in 323 B.C. He was the notable horn between the eyes of the he goat. This was a detail not mentioned in either chapters 2 or 7 of the book of Daniel. However, the prophecy enlarges further, declaring that four notable horns arose after the demise of Alexander.

> Therefore the he goat waxed very great: and when he was strong, the great horn was broken; and for it came up four notable ones toward the four winds of heaven. (Daniel 8:8)

> Now that being broken, whereas four stood up for it, four kingdoms shall stand up out of the nation, but not in his power. (Daniel 8:22)

After Alexander's death there was turmoil in which a number of claimants to the throne were assassinated. Eventually, the four powerful generals divided the Greek kingdom into four regions. Ptolemy became the king of the South, ruling Egypt, Palestine, and part of Syria. Cassander became king of the West (Macedonia). Lysimachus ruled Thrace and Greece as king of the North. Seleucus ruled much of Syria, Mesopotamia, and the east as king of the East. How precise is the interpretation of this divine prophecy!

There is need for further explanation to understand the term "toward the four winds of heaven." This is a difficult passage for Hebrew scholars to interpret, as the Hebrew language is ambiguous so that "out of one of them" could mean either out of one of the four *winds* or out of one of the four *horns*. As this little horn clearly refers to Rome (paralleling the little horn of chapter 7), one of the four *winds* would easily fit the understanding, for Rome did not arise out of any of the four divisions of the Greek Empire. Thus if it refers to the four *winds*, meaning in the concrete language of Hebrew that it reflects the four points of the compass, it is easily understood.

This little horn is first referred to in Daniel 7:8.

> I considered the horns, and, behold, there came up among them another little horn, before whom there were three of the first horns plucked up by the roots: and, behold, in this horn were eyes like the eyes of man, and a mouth speaking great things. (Daniel 7:8)

In Daniel 7:8 the little horn rises out of the pagan Roman Empire and clearly identifies the rise of papal Rome. In chapter 8, the little horn is identified as Rome in both its pagan and papal form, no doubt because papal Rome took up and incorporated into its form of Christianity many pagan doctrines and practices of pagan Rome. It will be noted that this little horn "waxed exceeding great," thus more powerful than either the Medo-Persian Empire or the Greek Empire, and certainly that was true of both of the pagan Roman Empire (164 B.C.–476 A.D.) and papal Rome (538–1798).

> And out of one of them came forth a little horn, which waxed exceeding great, toward the south, and toward the east, and toward the pleasant land. (Daniel 8:9)

Both pagan and papal forms of Rome were responsible for fearful slaughters and persecution and also strongly defied the veracity of God and His truth and righteousness. It is plain that this little horn power will continue to focus its persecution upon God's faithful followers.

> And in the latter time of their kingdom, when the transgressors are come to the full, a king of fierce countenance, and understanding dark sentences, shall stand up. And his power shall be mighty, but not by his own power: and he shall destroy wonderfully, and shall prosper, and practise, and shall destroy the mighty and the holy people. (Daniel 8:23–24)

It will be noted that the papal Roman power will stand against the "Prince of princes"—a clear reference to Christ Himself.

> And through his policy also he shall cause craft to prosper in his hand; and he shall magnify himself in his heart, and by peace shall destroy many: he shall also stand up against the Prince of princes; but he shall be broken without hand. (Daniel 8:25)

However the papal power will be broken comprehensively and destroyed. This prophecy parallels the prophecy of John the Revelator which also predicts the utter destruction of the papacy before the return of our blessed Savior.

> And the ten horns which thou sawest upon the beast, these shall hate the whore [papal Rome], and shall make her desolate and naked, and shall eat her flesh, and burn her with fire. (Revelation 17:16)

At the time of the death of Pope John Paul II, the German weekly magazine *Der Spiegel* wrote extensively on the pope's death and the history of the papacy. In commenting on the papal history, it used the biblical word "whore" to describe the medieval papacy and its ruthless rulership:

> For more than 1,500 years the political ideology of the identity of religion and society controlled the Western world. The Catholic Church became the queen of politics and the whore of the leaders. For more than 1,000 years she fought, led by her pontiff, more or less successfully, to dominate society. Whoever did not follow the beliefs and commands of the pope lost political status and risked his personal existence and his life. The pope and his bishops controlled the direction [of the Western world]. (Smoltczyk, et. al., *Der Spiegel*, Germany's leading news magazine, April 11, 2005, p. 101; translated to English)

This is yet another prophecy with precise details which has withstood the attacks of the skeptics.

All that remains now of the prophecy of Daniel 8 to be fulfilled is the ultimate destruction of this little horn power, the papacy. We pray that all readers will submit their wills to Christ so comprehensively that none will be destroyed when the papacy is destroyed.

CHAPTER 7
The Papal Deadly Wound

SIR Isaac Newton, (1642–1727), of Cambridge University, was arguably the greatest physicist and mathematician in known history. Some believe he was even greater than Albert Einstein, who acknowledged his indebtedness to Newton and expressed doubts that the great advances in knowledge he had achieved could have taken place had it not been for the discoveries and insights of Newton.

Newton was a faithful believer in the Bible and in prophecy. Besides being a great scientist, he was a great theologian in the purest sense of the word. Indeed, he wrote more on prophecy than upon science. Unlike Newton, Albert Einstein and Stephen Hawking (who is presently the Lucasian Professor at Cambridge University, once occupied by Newton) both rejected the infallible Word of God. Like most Protestants of his generation, Newton clearly identified the papacy as the beast power of Revelation 13:1–10. Unlike most expositors of the book of Revelation today, whose minds have been warped within the framework of ecumenism, Newton understood that this first power of Revelation 13 was the enemy of truth and righteousness. Newton lived close enough to the middle ages to realize the fearful persecution of this power, and he understood that before the return of Jesus, this same power would reestablish the same ruthless suppression of those who stood in the path of its authority. Of course, Newton did not live to see the fulfillment of that prophecy. Certainly he saw nothing of the fulfillment of Revelation 13:3. The text reads as follows,

> And I saw one of his heads as it were wounded to death; and his deadly wound was healed: and all the world wondered after the beast. (Revelation 13:3)

> But it [the little horn of Daniel 7] was a kingdom of a different kind from the other ten kingdoms [referred to in Daniel 7:7–8], having a life or soul peculiar to itself, with eyes and a mouth. By its eyes it was a Seer; and by its mouth speaking great things and changing times and laws, it was a Prophet as well as a King. . . . And such a Seer, a Prophet and a King, is the Church of Rome. (Sir Isaac Newton, *Observations on the Prophecies*, p. 75)

This intriguing prophecy, it will be noted, has three distinct parts to it:

1. And I saw one of his heads as it were wounded to death
2. And his deadly wound was healed
3. And all the world wondered after the beast

It has taken until this time in history for that prophecy to be completely fulfilled. In an amazing way all three statements have been fulfilled by the papacy. This fulfillment fully affirms Newton's identification of the papacy's rulership. Just prior to the return of our Savior, this beast power will rule over all the inhabitants of the world, with the exception of those who are God's faithful people whose names are written in the Lamb's book of life.

> And all that dwell upon the earth shall worship him, whose names are not written in the book of life of the Lamb slain from the foundation of the world. (Revelation 13:8)

Returning to verse three, the examination of history is a fascinating example of the pinpoint accuracy of biblical prophecy. Regarding point one, this prophecy foretold that the papacy would experience a deadly wound.

The Bible even foretold the year in which this would happen. Indeed, seven times its lengthy reign was set in concrete. It is the prophecy of the 1,260 years of papal domination of Europe. Here are the seven verses:

> And he shall speak great words against the most High, and shall wear out the saints of the most High, and think to change times and laws: and they shall be given into his hand until *a time and times and the dividing of time.* (Daniel 7:25)

> And I heard the man clothed in linen, which was upon the waters of the river, when he held up his right hand and his left hand unto heaven, and sware by him that liveth for ever that it shall be for *a time, times, and an half;* and when he shall have accomplished to scatter the power of the holy people, all these things shall be finished. (Daniel 12:7)

> But the court which is without the temple leave out, and measure it not; for it is given unto the Gentiles: and the holy city shall they tread under foot *forty and two months.* (Revelation 11:2)

> And I will give power unto my two witnesses, and they shall prophesy *a thousand two hundred and threescore days*, clothed in sackcloth. (Revelation 11:3)

> And the woman fled into the wilderness, where she hath a place prepared of God, that they should feed her there *a thousand two hundred and threescore days.* (Revelation 12:6)

> And to the woman were given two wings of a great eagle, that she might fly into the wilderness, into her place, where she is nourished for *a time, and times, and half a time*, from the face of the serpent. (Revelation 12:14)

> And there was given unto him a mouth speaking great things and blasphemies; and power was given unto him to continue *forty and two months*. (Revelation 13:5)

Now at first it may not occur to the occasional reader of Bible prophecy that these seven prophetic utterances each deal with the papacy as a persecuting and controlling power, or that all verses are dealing with exactly the same time period of 1,260 years.

You see, in Daniel 7:25, "a time" was the equivalent of a year, "times" represented two years, and the "dividing of time" represented half a year, or all together, three and a half years. With Daniel 12:7, only slightly different words are used, "time, times, and an half," and it is also referenced to Revelation 12:14.

In Revelation 11:2, the term "forty and two months" is used. The ancient Jewish calendar comprised 12 months, each of 30 days. The Jews understood this very well, for it was the language which was familiar to them. Taking the 30 days of each month of the Jewish calendar, 42 months translates into 1,260 days. Confirming this is the fact that this time period is referenced in the margin of some Bibles. Revelation 11:2 is referenced to Revelation 13:5 where "forty and two months" is employed, and Revelation 11:3 is linked with Revelation 12:6, both of which express the same period of time as "a thousand two hundred and threescore days."

Whether the Bible is addressing three and half years, forty-two months, or 1,260 days, it is the same time period. However, as is the case in prophecy, the numbers are literal, but they are attached to symbolic objects or periods. Frequently in Bible prophecy, a day represents a year. Thus, when 1,260 days are mentioned, they are symbolic of 1,260 years. There are a couple of Scriptural examples to support this which we have referenced before.

> After the number of the days in which ye searched the land, even forty days, each day for a year, shall ye bear your iniquities, even forty years, and ye shall know my breach of promise. (Numbers 14:34)

> And when thou hast accomplished them, lie again on thy right side, and thou shalt bear the iniquity of the house of Judah forty days: I have appointed thee each day for a year. (Ezekiel 4:6)

There are other prophecies in the Bible which are just the same. In the prophecy of Daniel 8:14, 2,300 days represent a period of 2,300 years. When converted into days, the prophetic weeks of Daniel 9 translate into years. For some, this may be new and may sound a little complicated, but in reality it is not difficult. (See chapter entitled, "The Years of Christ's Ministry and Sacrifice Foretold")

Historical research has to be undertaken to determine when the period of 1,260 years took place. Clearly, it is a period of great domination, when the Roman Catholic Church had the power to persecute those who would not support the gross apostasy and false practices of the Roman Catholic Church. A careful study of history leads to the date 538, when Pope Vigilius was the reigning pope, as the commencement of this 1,260-year period. (See Heidi Heikes, *508 538 1798 1843 Source Book* [Knoxville, IL: Hope International, 2007], p. 39)

Five years earlier, in 533, Emperor Justinian of the Eastern Roman Empire declared the bishop of Rome, Pope John II, as the preeminent bishop of the Christian Church. This decree was to settle the dispute in favor of Rome rather than Constantinople as to which city was the first bishopric of the Catholic Church. However, because the Ostrogoths had overrun Rome, the opportunity of the pope to exercise his power did not take place until five years later, in 538, when the Ostrogoths were driven out of Rome and Vigilius was the reigning pope. Also in 538, the Council of Orleans was conducted in France at which it was commanded that all Christians must keep holy the first day of the week rather than God's seventh-day Sabbath. This decree was enforced by severe penalties for violations by the civil authorities. Now, once the beginning date of 538 is established, it does not take a specialist mathematician to know when the deadly wound would be inflicted which would completely end the medieval reign of the papacy. Adding 1,260 years, detailed in the seven prophecies found in Daniel and Revelation, brings us to 1798. Did this prophecy have a fulfillment in that year? It certainly did. Let us look at the events leading up to the end of the medieval reign of the papacy.

In the century or two before 1798, the power of the papacy was in great decline. Even the Roman Catholic-dominated nations were no longer the servants of the papacy. Of course, the Protestant reformation of the sixteenth century had made a deep dent in the authority of the papacy. However, let us see how this prophecy was perfectly fulfilled.

One year before the end of the 1,260-year prophecy, the reigning pope was Pius VI. At the time he was the longest reigning pope in history, although three popes subsequently have reigned longer than he reigned. In 1797, one year before the end of the 1,260-year prophecy, Pope Pius VI, then in his 80s, fell desperately ill. So desperate was his physical condition that physicians gave up all hope of his recovery.

At that time, Italy was not a united nation, being made up of many small states. The Napoleonic Wars began soon after this time, and Napoleon had already subjugated the small Italian states and had placed his brother Joseph Bonaparte as the ruler of this region. When Joseph Bonaparte learned that the pope would soon die, he quickly sent a message to the directorate (parliament, or congress) of France, reporting the grave condition of the pope and asking for instructions as quickly as possible. The instructions came back that, when the pope died, he was not to permit another pope to be elected. Atheistic France was determined to end forever religion and the papacy.

However, if Pope Pius VI had died in 1797, the 1,260-year prophecy would have been in error by one year, and the Bible, because it is the inspired Word of God, does not make such mistakes. Indeed, against every prediction of his physicians, Pius VI recovered and rose to a degree of health from what was thought to have been his deathbed. This recovery greatly frustrated Joseph Bonaparte and the French government.

At the same time, many of these Italian states were becoming restless against the subjugation of the Napoleonic forces. Thus Napoleon sent one of his finest generals, General Berthier, to quell the insurrections. He was given a commission that once he reached Rome, he was to demand the abdication of the pope; otherwise, if the pope refused, he was to take the pope prisoner. When the army of Berthier reached Rome, he sent a number of his senior officers, who found the pope kneeling before the altar in St. Peter's basilica. The army officers demanded his resignation; however, in spite of the fact that he was old, weak, and sickly, the pope refused. So, it would seem, rather gently, they took him prisoner and removed his fisherman's ring—the insignia of his papal authority. After a four-month staged journey, he was in France as a captive, living in a comfortable villa.

Secular historians such as George Trevor declared the papacy extinct and pointed out that not one of the Roman Catholic nations of Europe lifted a finger to assist the hapless papacy.

> The object of the French directory was the destruction of the pontifical government, as the irreconcilable enemy of the republic. . . . The aged pope [Pius VI] was summoned to surrender the temporal government; on his refusal, he was dragged from the altar. . . . His rings were torn from his fingers, and finally, after declaring the temporal power abolished, the victors carried the pope prisoner into Tuscany, whence he never returned (1798).
>
> The Papal States, converted into the *Roman Republic*, were declared to be in perpetual alliance with France, but the French general was the real master at Rome. . . . The territorial possessions of the clergy and monks were declared national property, and their former owners cast into prison. The papacy was extinct: not a vestige of its existence remained; and among all the Roman Catholic powers not a finger was stirred in its defence. The Eternal City had no longer prince or pontiff; its bishop was a dying captive in foreign lands; and the decree was already announced that no successor would be allowed in his place. (*Rome: From the Fall of the Western Empire* [London: The Religious Tract Society, 1868], pp. 439–440)

Here was the deadly wound. Here was the end of the medieval reign of the papacy. France was determined that the papacy would never again be reestablished. Pius VI was taken prisoner February 15, 1798. Thus was fulfilled, to the very year, the 1,260-year reign of the medieval papacy. There were to be two more aspects to the papacy, however, which the French had not regarded, probably because of their determination to destroy all the Bibles in France. They had no idea that the prophecy of God had said that the deadly wound would be healed. For it to be healed, the papacy had to be reestablished, and indeed, it certainly was. The Bible never fails.

After the death of Pius VI, secretly the emperor of the Austro-Hungarian Empire let word be known to some of the cardinals that he would support them if they elected another pope. Indeed, they did so, the new pope taking the name of Pius VII. Including Pope Pius VII, there have now been, at the time of writing, fifteen popes up to and including Benedict XVI since the deadly wound. The unfailing Word of God, the sure word of prophecy, said that the deadly wound would be healed. It seemed, however, even many decades after the wound, that the reestablishment of the papacy's power seemed remote, that this prophecy would fail, and fail miserably. Indeed, in 1870, another terrible setback overtook the papacy.

Under the leadership of Garibaldi in 1870, all the states of Italy united. These included the five papal states which had been directly under the rulership of the papacy. Now not one grain of soil belonged to the papacy. So devastated by this was Pope Pius IX, that he declared that he would not leave the Vatican's 108.7 acres until sovereignty was returned to the Vatican. Sovereignty did not return in his lifetime, and eight years later, in 1878, he died, having been self-imprisoned within the borders of the Vatican. As late as the latter part of the nineteenth and early twentieth century, historians both Protestant and Roman Catholic agreed that the papacy was very weak and was unlikely ever to regain its former glory.

> The conviction had been widely and confidently expressed by writers, thinkers, and politicians across Europe—Bovio [Catholic] in Italy, Balzac [Catholic] in France, Bismarck [Protestant] in Germany, Gladstone [Protestant] in England—that the Papacy, and Catholicism

with it, had had its day. (John Cornwell, *Hitler's Pope: the Secret History of Pius XII* [London: Penguin Books, 1999], p. 14–15)

How wrong these historians and politicians were! They did not take into account the inerrant words of Revelation 13:3: "and the deadly wound was healed." That healing began and has continued ever since February 11, 1929.

This healing began when the ambitious prime minister of Italy, Benito Mussolini, signed the Lateran Treaty, giving back to the papacy its territory, the Vatican—those 108.7 acres. Thus was reestablished the Vatican again as a sovereign nation amongst the nations of the world. Most historians agree that Mussolini did not appear to be aiming to reestablish the power of the Vatican. However, this was his gift in an attempt to ingratiate himself to the Vatican and gain the support of Roman Catholics as he developed his dictatorship in Italy. The very next day, February 12, 1929, the *San Francisco Chronicle* confirmed the words of Scripture, that the deadly wound was healed. Reporting upon the Lateran Treaty, which was signed by Benito Mussolini on behalf of King Victor Emmanuel III, king of Italy, and Cardinal Gaspari, representing Pope Pius XI, the *San Francisco Chronicle* included in its article headlines these words, "Heal Wound of Many Years." The very words of Scripture were confirmed by the secular press. (To learn much more about what led up to 1929 and the Lateran Treaty, and what has taken place since, see our book *Two Beasts, Three Deadly Wounds, and Fifteen Popes*. Available at Hartland Publications [see back page for address].)

However, the third part of the Revelation 13:3 prophecy was still to be fulfilled.

> . . . all the world wondered after the beast. (Revelation 13:3)

Clearly in 1929 that had not been achieved. Upon the death of Pius XI, Pius XII was elected pope. Indeed, his was one of the most controversial pontificates of modern times. As lads growing up, we well remember Pope

Pius XII. As Cardinal Pacelli, he had been papal nuncio to Nazi Germany. He was believed to be anti-Semitic, and he was greatly suspicioned, during World War II, of being sympathetic to the Nazi and Fascist causes. (See our book, *Antichrist Is Here*, pp. 91–92. Available from Hartland Publications.) Many (including many Roman Catholics) believed that he sought an alliance with Hitler's Nazi Germany. Certainly, this pope was despised or even hated by millions around the world. However, the climate of public opinion began to change with his successor, John XXIII, who called the Second Vatican Council (1962–1965).

The Second Vatican Council began a process which was dramatically and brilliantly enhanced during the long pontificate of Pope John Paul II. With great amazement, many watched as this pope wooed the masses of the world—not only Roman Catholics, but also Protestants, leaders of non-Christian religions, and even many secular leaders who had little or no religious affiliation. This rise to popularity has brought the papacy to the fulfillment of the third part of this one-verse prophecy:

> . . . all the world wondered after the beast. (Revelation 13:3)

Many news organizations in deep amazement reported that perhaps John Paul II was more powerful in his death than even during his spectacular life. The fact that the flags of many Protestant organizations were lowered to half mast on the death of the pope indicated a dramatic change—a gigantic shift towards the dismantling of Protestantism. John Paul II's influence was not limited to the Catholics and other Christian churches. Jews, Muslims, Hindus, Buddhists, and other religious leaders paid homage to him. This adulation extended to the great men of the secular world as seen when they knelt before the bier of the deceased pontiff.

The grandeur of the many services connected with the burial of the pope resulted in the *Sydney Morning Herald* (Australia) publishing these amazing words about the funeral.

> It was magnificent and humbling and filled with *wonderment*. (April 9–10 weekend edition)

Those words fulfilled the third part of Revelation 13:3,

> . . . and all the world *wondered* after the beast.

It took 207 years from the deadly wound of the papacy in 1798 until the secular media acknowledged the reestablishment of the mesmeric influence of the papacy over the people of the world.

We will soon see the fulfillment of Revelation 13:8, which says that

> . . . all that dwell upon the earth shall worship him, whose names are not written in the book of life of the Lamb slain from the foundation of the world.

What a serious time this is! What a momentous period we have reached in the final moments of this earth's history before the coming of our blessed Lord and Savior! However, let us remember that only God's saints will stand against this apostate power. Yes, it took 207 years to complete the prophecy of this one verse, but how reliable is God's precious Word! The agnostics, atheists, skeptics, and infidels of the past did not have the wealth of information regarding more recent biblical prophetic fulfillments as is available today. Their skepticism today surely is unjustifiable with these startling modern-day fulfillments.

CHAPTER 8
An Eight-Word Question and the Fate of a Nation

WE were five years old when the young prime minister of Australia, Robert Gordon Menzies, committed Australia to the conflict that was soon to become known as World War II. About ten hours after Great Britain declared war on Nazi Germany after the German army invaded Poland, the Australian Prime Minister uttered these cryptic words, "Great Britain is at war; therefore, Australia is at war."

In that era, that seemed the only thing to do, for Australia was devotedly loyal to the "mother country." Young though we were, we grasped at least to some extent that something very serious was taking place. That fateful day was September 3, 1939. In July 1939, our family had moved to Cardiff, a small town about seven miles south of our birth city of Newcastle. At the Cardiff public school we had been placed in the first grade.

For the next six years the war dominated our understanding of what the world was. It was not a world of peace and tranquility. Indeed, it was a world of tension and increasing fear which greatly increased dramatically when the might of the Japanese air force attacked Pearl Harbor on December 7, 1941. Soon we realized that the Japanese military had a determined goal to attack Australia and occupy our island continent.

Big changes took place. Our father dug and constructed an air-raid shelter in our side yard. Huge trenches were dug around the perimeter of our school. We had drills to run quickly to the trenches if it would be needed. We were trained to lie flat on the ground whenever an airplane came into view without seeking to identify whether it was a friendly airplane or of enemy origin. Australia then had a population of about seven million in a land mass about the same area as the 48 contiguous states of the USA. Had not the might of the United States navy eventually overcome the Japanese navy, Australia almost certainly would have been vanquished by the might of the military forces of Imperial Japan.

As the war progressed, the Allied forces appeared to face a desperate challenge as the Axis powers of Germany and its supporting nations seemed likely to overrun Europe. France, Belgium, and the Netherlands were overrun with consummate ease before the overwhelming force of the German power. It seemed that any moment the Germans would cross the English Channel to engulf the United Kingdom, but by the beginning of 1943, the fortunes of war began to change. On the eastern front, the German armies in the Soviet Union began to falter before the ferocious resistance of the Soviet military and the unforgiving cold of the Russian winter. Further, the American military began to make its presence felt both in the Pacific and the European sphere of conflict, shifting the balance of power toward the Allied nations.

Another issue was changing the picture of this devastating war. Increasing unrest turned the majority of Italy's populace against Italy's involvement in the war and against the dictatorial leadership of that nation's Prime Minister, Benito Mussolini. By 1943, the Italians were retreating, and its soldiers were surrendering in alarming numbers to the Allied forces, especially in North Africa. It became obvious that the Italians had no stomach to continue a war which had already spilt the blood of too many of the cream of the young men of that nation.

Yet, it is this situation which caused a greater focus upon the nation of Italy and the strategies employed by the Allies in the war they were staging against this nation. This focus was to be the basis of a dramatic presentation at an evangelistic crusade which was conducted in Lambton, a suburb of Newcastle, Australia. We were now nine years old and were living with our grandfather who was recently widowed, in Hamilton, the suburb of Newcastle where we were born.

This crusade was presented by a dynamic speaker, Edwin Jewson. Evangelist Jewson, an Englishman, came in a small package of short stature, but he was a powerful exponent of the Bible. Strategically, the white tent where this crusade was conducted was close to the tram (street car) line. Each night of the crusade, our family would travel by tram to the meetings. The chairs were not so comfortable. The earthen floor was covered with saw-dust, and the tent was heated by kerosene burners. (There were no fire-codes in those days to prevent this.) Primitive though the facility was, it was adequate and acceptable, at least during war time in Australian history.

One night the topic was especially intriguing. The title simply asked the question, "Why No Bombs on Rome?" Evangelist Jewson enlightened the attendees that, despite the fact that the Americans had bases in the Sahara desert of North Africa from which they raided cities in Italy such as Naples, Milan, and Turin, the Allied air forces (both the British and the U.S. air forces) had dropped no bombs on the city of Rome.

Why no bombs on Rome? Apparently this was a well-reasoned decision by the leaders of the Allies. It was argued that the risk was too great. To bomb Rome could create a public relations disaster should even one bomb "stray" from its target and destroy part of the Vatican. Remember, the skills of bombardiers varied greatly, especially when many crews had little combat experience. Also, remember, there were no "smart" guided missiles in that era. The raids were made during the darkness of night, and, of course, every possible light in Rome was shaded to greatly reduce the visibility of targets from enemy aircraft.

We can only imagine what would have been the response if the Vatican would have been damaged. What if Saint Peter's Basilica, the magnificent Vatican cathedral, had been destroyed or if the reigning pope would have been killed? So demoralized would have been the Roman Catholic citizens of the Allied countries that the Allies with understandable caution decided not to bomb Rome.

Now what has all this to do with biblical prophecy? There are a few prophetic words in Revelation chapter 13 at the end of verse 4 which are at stake. Here are the words in context. Note the last eight words.

> And I saw one of his heads as it were wounded to
> death; and his deadly wound was healed: and all the world

> wondered after the beast. And they worshipped the dragon which gave power unto the beast: and they worshipped the beast, saying, Who is like unto the beast? *who is able to make war with him*? (Revelation 13:3–4)

Note that the "him" refers to the first beast of Revelation 13, which many Protestant Reformers centuries before had identified as the papacy. Many converted Christians in the 1940s still believed that identification. Of course, the papacy is located in the smallest nation in the world—the Vatican. The second question of Revelation 13:4 is a rhetorical question, with the obvious implications that no nation is able to make war with the papacy.

This is such an amazing prophecy! Virtually any other small nation would have no problem conquering this state of 108.7 acres and less than 1,000 inhabitants. Yet the Vatican is arguably the safest country in the world. It is not surprising that the Allied nations were determined to protect it at all cost. We believe that few, if any, of those who made the decision not to bomb Rome had any knowledge that their decision was helping to fulfill this prophecy. One thing must be understood, Revelation 13:4 deals with the papacy's history after the deadly wound was healed as stated in Revelation 13:3. (See chapter entitled "The Papal Deadly Wound.") However, the book of Revelation does indicate that very shortly before the return of Jesus the papacy will be terribly destroyed.

> And the ten horns which thou sawest are ten kings, which have received no kingdom as yet; but receive power as kings one hour [a short period of time] with the beast. These have one mind, and shall give their power and strength unto the beast. These shall make war with the Lamb, and the Lamb shall overcome them: for he is Lord of lords, and King of kings: and they that are with him are called, and chosen, and faithful. . . . And the ten horns which thou sawest upon the beast, these shall hate the whore, and shall make her desolate and naked, and shall eat her flesh, and burn her with fire. For God hath

put in their hearts to fulfil his will, and to agree, and give their kingdom unto the beast, until the words of God shall be fulfilled. (Revelation 17:12–14, 16–17)

What a tragic ending this will be to the once-powerful papacy, the wonderment of the world! Of course, this end of the papacy is yet future.

We would warn against a contemporary tendency to suggest that the first beast of Revelation 13 is possibly Islam. Obviously, with the Afghan and Iraqi wars, Islam has shown its tenacity against the might of the United States and its allies. But those who propose Islam rather than the papacy certainly reject the identification of the Reformers who carefully researched the Scriptures and left the papacy as the only power which could fulfill all the characteristics of this beast power. Certainly these eight words of Revelation 13:4 ("who is able to make war with him?") could not be fulfilled by Islam. In the Six Day War, Israel victoriously attacked Egypt; the Soviets in the 1980s unsuccessfully attacked Afghanistan; and the United States has attacked both Afghanistan and Iraq. Let our readers not spend a moment on this false theory, but let all acknowledge the remarkable fulfillment of this prophecy of eight impactful words.

Chapter 9
The Fall of Communism

WHEN we were growing up in Newcastle, Australia, we thought little of communism. Of course we had heard of it, but the Soviet Union was on "our side" during World War II. We certainly thought much concerning the evils of Nazi Germany and Fascist Italy, for they were "the enemy." We were just short of our sixth birthday when Australia declared war against Germany in loyal support of the mother country—Great Britain. After all, at that time more than ninety-five percent of Australians were British-Irish. We were exceptions. While our genes were mostly English, Irish, and Scottish, we knew that, unlike most Australians, we had a significant minority of genes from our German ancestors. Of course, having an English family name gave no hint of our German heritage, and during the Second World War there seemed little advantage to mention our German forebears, for now Germany was the adversary.

On December 7, 1941, when the Japanese air force attacked the United States' fleet at Pearl Harbor, there now came a much more feared threat to Australia. While it was largely the American army, navy, and air force upon which Australia had to depend for its defense, we saw the Soviets as allies on the "good side," for they had joined forces against the Axis powers led by Germany. We remember talking to our next-door neighbor lady, when we were no more than eight years old, about how wonderful it was that we had the Soviets to fight against the Germans, for already they were making things difficult for the Germans.

It was not until some time after the war ended that our maturing minds began to realize we no longer looked at the Soviets as our allies; now they were "our enemy." Ever more alarming, communism, like a prairie fire, was rapidly expanding around the world. Not one continent, with the exception of our own continent nation Australia and North America, was without serious threat from the communist expansion. Even in Australia, one communist candidate won a seat in the Queensland State Parliament to the alarm of most Australians. Yet, though very vocal, the communists remained a very small group.

However, it was not so in Africa, Europe, Asia, and South and Central America. All Eastern Europe was engulfed by communism. In Africa, countries such as Tanganyika (now Tanzania) and Angola were greatly attracted to the communist doctrine. In Latin America, Cuba, Nicaragua, Chile, El Salvador, and many other countries were under communist influence. However, it was in Asia that the greatest threat developed. Much of India was attracted to its philosophy. Communist insurgents were strong in the Philippines, Malaysia, Thailand, North Korea, North Vietnam, Cambodia and Laos. The latter three countries rapidly became engulfed by communist governments.

The Asian threat was especially alarming to Australians. During World War II, Australians had felt intense pressure of what many called "the yellow peril." This resulted from the realistic fear of an imminent take-over of Australia by the powerful Imperial Army of Japan. Australian hearts failed when in 1942 the Japanese took control of the British fortress of Singapore with ridiculous ease, notwithstanding the confident assurances that Australia had received from the British that the island's defenses were impregnable.

Well we remember that day, though we were but eight years of age. That fateful night, our worried father, Darcy Roland Standish, tuned our big cabinet St. James radio to the short-wave broadcast from Radio Japan, as he occasionally did. For some time the Japanese had beamed English broadcasts to the Australian people, no doubt to fill their hearts with great fear. In this they were very successful.

However, this night greatly increased the Australian concerns many fold as we listened to what could only be described as outrageous bragging. In almost perfect English, the news reporter spoke of the British claims to invincibility, while the mighty Imperial Army of Japan

The Fall of Communism

had caused all opposition from enemy fire to cease in a few short days. Well we remember the final chilling comments at the conclusion of the broadcast: "Now it is on to the Dutch East Indies [Indonesia] and then to Australia." Even two little eight year olds could not escape the fear which these words engendered in their minds.

By the mercy of God this "yellow peril" did not reach Australia. However, the peace of mind the Australian populace felt at the conclusion of World War II was not permitted a long respite from such a threat. Rapidly after the end of World War II, an even greater threat than Japan arose. This came from China, as communism was swiftly overrunning the length and breadth of that country. The existing government, under the Kuomintang Party lead by Chiang Kai-shek, was rapidly driven out of mainland China to establish a government in exile on the island of Taiwan. When in 1951 the communists took control over Shanghai, to all intents and purposes communism was in control of the whole nation of China. Led by Mao Tse-tung, one of the original founders of the Communist Party in China in 1921, China could now claim to be the largest communist nation on the planet. Calling itself the People's Republic of China, it soon assumed a growing threat to the democracies of the world. Almost half the population of the world was either under communist rule or at least greatly threatened by it.

You may be wondering what all this has to do with the fulfillment of impossible biblical prophecy. Please be patient with us. Let us now return to Australia. Australians had barely settled down from the fearful threat of the Japanese, and now their eyes and ears were glued to the developing threat of yet another "yellow peril," much larger, driven now by the communist ideology. Paranoia returned to Australia. In 1952, the Australian population was inching up close to nine million in a land mass approximately the same area as the continental 48 states of the United States. A year later in 1953, a national census showed China had a population of more than 582 million. By contrast, at this time, the population of Japan was no more than 90 million. Long had Australians suspicioned that one day the masses of Asians to the north would envy the open spaces of Australia as an ideal place to off-load some of their bulging populations by whatever means they needed to employ.

63

..stralians were already strongly concerned with communism, but while it was far removed in Europe and other scattered parts of the world, it was not seen as posing an immediate threat to Australia. Yet now it seemed that from India around the Pacific Coast of Asia to Korea, communism was on the march. Some Australians acted as if Australia was like a helpless infant waiting for the Asian tigers to pounce. By this time, it was not uncommon to hear Australians express the thought that communism was unstoppable and that one day, sooner rather than later, communism would control the whole world. An increasing pessimism was growing amongst many Australians, even a deep resignation to "the inevitable." Not even the United States, it was thought, could ultimately stand against this irresistible force.

The Kennedy years in the United States only gave great credence to this pessimism. By this time, the Americans had not been able to stop the building of the Berlin Wall. Yes, Kennedy used much rhetoric while standing at the wall, but that did not remove a grain of sand from the wall.

America had launched a war against the North Vietnamese, and it was soon discerned that the might of the United States seemed powerless to defeat this rather small communist state. It was then becoming known that the Soviets had a much larger army, a much bigger navy, and a bigger air force than the United States. It outnumbered the Americans in tanks and most other military hardware.

The bungled Bay of Pigs offensive of 1961 involved an invading force, approved by the Kennedy administration, which attempted to overthrow Castro's communist government, but it was roundly defeated. America's capacity to stand toe to toe with world-wide communism was in grave doubt. It seemed that the most powerful nation of the Western world was no match for the power of communism. The USA seemed impotent even to handle a small nation located on its door step.

However, another great shock had already come with the successful launch of Sputnik 1, on October 4, 1957. So advanced was this spacecraft that it successfully orbited once around the earth. However, when on April 12, 1961, Russian cosmonaut Yuri Gagarin became the first human in known history to orbit the earth in a spaceship, the Soviets were seen to be far ahead of the Americans in space technology. Most unconvincing was the American's launch of its astronaut, Alan Shepard, into a fifteen minute sub-orbital flight the following month in a desperate effort to lift the spirits of a demoralized Western world. Indeed, all it did was prove beyond any doubt that Soviet scientists were significantly ahead of their American counterparts.

Are you still wondering what all this has to do with biblical prophecy? At last we have come to the point. In 1951, when gloom was spreading around Australia, a crusade was conducted in a tent in our home city of Newcastle by George Burnside, a New Zealander. One day, the banner advertising the meeting for that night was emblazoned with the words, "Why Communism Cannot Rule the World." We were then seventeen years of age. For us, it was a meeting we could not miss. It certainly captured our attention and also a sizeable crowd of interested citizens of our city.

Intensely we listened to the evangelist, who proceeded to show that there was no place for communism in the end-time prophecies of the Bible. His presentation was convincing to Bible believers. We suppose that those who did not possess confidence in God's Word might have dismissed the presentation as of no merit. After all, the evidence was that the United States and her allies were losing the war of words, the "Cold War." The evidence was that day by day communism was increasing its reach around the world, notwithstanding the huge budget set aside by the U.S. Congress to seek to catch up.

To which prophecy did this evangelist turn to support his position? It was the prophecy of Revelation 13, which describes two beasts which will hold sway on the planet just prior to the return of Christ. By identifying the two beasts of Revelation 13, the Soviet Union (communism) was excluded as being a major player at the end of this world's history as we know it. To Bible believing youth, the evangelist's presentation was compelling to us.

The first beast, which appeared like a leopard, had been identified by many prophecy expositors especially in the eighteenth and nineteenth centuries as the papacy. Briefly, here are a few of the evidences that we find in Revelation 13:

Verse 1. "Rise up out of the sea"
It had to have arisen in the more densely populated part of the world, which limited it to Southern Europe, Asia and Northern Africa, as waters represent large numbers of people.

> And he saith unto me, The waters which thou sawest, where the whore sitteth, are peoples, and multitudes, and nations, and tongues. (Revelation 17:15)

The papacy arose in the Mediterranean region in the sixth century where, at that time, there was one of the highest concentrations of human beings on the planet.

Verse 1. "Upon his heads the name of blasphemy."

Many protestant expositors had discovered two forms of blasphemy in the Bible.

A. Claiming to be God

> But Jesus held his peace. And the high priest answered and said unto him, I adjure thee by the living God, that thou tell us whether thou be the Christ, the Son of God. Jesus saith unto him, Thou hast said: nevertheless I say unto you, Hereafter shall ye see the Son of man sitting on the right hand of power, and coming in the clouds of heaven. Then the high priest rent his clothes, saying, He hath spoken blasphemy; what further need have we of witnesses? behold, now ye have heard his blasphemy. (Matthew 26:63–65)

B. Claiming to be able to forgive sin

> And, behold, they brought to him a man sick of the palsy, lying on a bed: and Jesus seeing their faith said unto the sick of the palsy; Son, be of good cheer; thy sins be forgiven thee. And, behold, certain of the scribes said within themselves, This man blasphemeth. (Matthew 9:2–3)

The Church of Rome makes these blasphemous claims.

Verse 2.

This beast was a composite of a leopard, bear, and lion. In the reverse order, they were the first three mighty kingdoms referred to in the prophecies of Daniel 7—the pagan kingdoms of Babylon, Medo-Persia, and Greece. (See chapter entitled, "Four Beasts, Ten Horns, and a Little Horn.") The composite beast of Revelation 13, though claiming to be a Christian power, has clearly included the pagan philosophies of the Babylonians, Medo-Persians and especially the Greeks. The history of the Roman Church is replete with evidence of the incorporation of pagan practices into the pure Christian faith. Just a few of these are infant baptism, indulgences, the rosary, Sunday sacredness, and an infallible leader who claims the title of God on earth. As Protestants readily recognized, no power on earth fitted these identifications other than the Roman Catholic Church.

Verse 3. "I saw one of his heads as it were wounded to death"

As we noted in the chapter entitled "The Papal Deadly Wound," verse 3 foretold that the papacy would suffer a deadly wound. On February 15, 1798 after a riot in Rome, the city was declared as a Republic. Pius VI and the curia were expelled, and later he was seized by the French and taken into exile in France where he died August 29, 1799. It was declared that the papacy was dead and that the Roman Catholic Church would soon vanish.

However, Scripture proceeds to declared that the deadly wound would be healed.

> And I saw one of his heads as it were wounded to death; and his deadly wound was healed: and all the world wondered after the beast. (Revelation 13:3)

The revival of the papacy is now for all to see. It has reached its influence all over the world. The Vatican was established as a sovereign nation of the world when the Lateran Treaty was signed, February 11, 1929, by Benito Mussolini for the Italian government and Pietro Cardinal Gaspari on behalf of the papacy. In the subsequent years which have followed, its influence in the world has expanded exponentially. (See chapter entitled "The Papal Deadly Wound.")

Verse 4. "Who is able to make war with him?"

Though the tiniest nation in the world, no nation dares to make war upon the Vatican. It was for this reason that Rome was not bombed by the Allies during the Second World War. The Allies were certain that should a bomb stray from its target to fall upon the Vatican, the negative ramifications would have been disastrous. (See chapter entitled "An Eight-Word Question and the Fate of a Nation.")

Verse 5. "Power was given unto him to continue forty and two months."

Using the Jewish calendar of biblical times, which had twelve months of thirty days each, "forty and two months" translate into 1,260 days. In Jewish prophecy, one prophetic day symbolized a literal year; thus, the 1,260 days represented 1,260 years—the exact number of years that the papal dominance of the Middle Ages continued until the deadly wound. (See chapter entitled "A Ram and a He Goat.") Once again, here are the texts that bear out the day-year principle of prophecy:

> And when thou hast accomplished them, lie again on thy right side, and thou shalt bear the iniquity of the house of Judah forty days: I have appointed thee each day for a year. (Ezekiel 4:6)

> After the number of the days in which ye searched the land, even forty days, each day for a year, shall ye bear your iniquities, even forty years, and ye shall know my breach of promise. (Numbers 14:34)

In 533, Emperor Justinian, of the Eastern Roman Empire, wrote to the Bishop of Rome, Pope John II, declaring him to be the head of all the churches. The popes, by an act of self-appropriation, had long before taken the religio-political title of Pontifex Maximus after the Roman

Emperor Gratian ceased to use that imperial title in 375. However, it was the year 538 when the bishop of Rome, now Pope Vigilius, was able to exercise the power bestowed by Justinian. In that year, the Ostrogoths were expelled from Rome, leaving the way open for the papacy to exert the temporal power claimed by the pope in his assumption of the title of Pontifex Maximus. This clearly is the commencement of the 1,260-year supremacy of the pope. With unerring accuracy, that period came to an end exactly 1,260 years later in 1798, when the then Pope Pius VI, was taken captive. Only the papacy fulfills this prophecy.

Verse 7. "Power to make war with the saints."

It is a tragic fact of history that tens of millions of Christians and others who refused to give their loyalty to the papacy lost their lives under the papal persecution and Inquisition. Some historians have estimated the number slain to be between fifty and one hundred and twenty million.

Verse 8.

> And all that dwell upon the earth shall worship him, whose names are not written in the book of life of the Lamb slain from the foundation of the world. (Revelation 13:8)

The time will come when all but the saints will worship this "beast." Already, the pope is recognized by many as the spiritual leader of the world. Many Protestants, including eminent men such as Billy Graham, have publicly acclaimed the pope as the spiritual and moral leader of the world. How their eyes have been blinded!

In that meeting in Newcastle in which the evangelist proposed to show "Why Communism Cannot Rule the World," after convincingly identifying the religio-political power of the papacy as the first great power at the end of the earth's history, he now set out to identify the second megapower, referred to as the second beast of Revelation 13:11–18.

This prophetic beast had defied identification until the middle of the nineteenth century when, by careful study, its identity was discerned by a young man from Maine, John Nevins Andrews. The evangelist of the Newcastle crusade in 1951 followed his reasoning. Below are the words which attracted the attention of Andrews and unlocked his understanding as to the identity of the second beast power.

Verse 11.

> And I beheld another beast coming up out of the earth; and he had two horns like a lamb, and he spake as a dragon. (Revelation 13:11)

1. This second beast came up out of the earth. Recognizing that the first beast came from the sea representing peoples and multitudes, he deducted that, by contrast, coming from the earth, the second mighty power had to arise out of a lightly populated part of the earth.
2. This beast had the characteristics of a young animal—a lamb. Andrews had noted that all the other beasts of prophecy, both in the Old and New Testaments, were mature animals—the lion, bear, leopard (of Daniel 7), and ram, and he-goat (of Daniel 8). Therefore, he logically concluded that this beast had to represent a young nation.

Using both these deductions, Andrews eliminated Europe, Asia, and Africa, leaving as the only possibility that it would be a new power which arose either in the Americas, in Australia, or in the South Pacific. He soon eliminated Australia and South and Central America and Canada, for they were not showing great strength, leaving only the new nation not yet 100 years old, the United States of America, as clearly this second beast of Revelation 13. It would become a great military-political power which would, at the end of this old world's history, enforce the edicts of the first beast, thus becoming a religio-political power and bringing all inhabitants of the world to worship this first beast power, the papacy.

When the evangelist spoke in the beginning of the 1950s, the fulfillment of this prophecy was not yet as evident as it is today. However,

The Fall of Communism

today the United States is unchallenged as the greatest military power in the world—so much so that, it could defy the will of most nations in the world and the United Nations when it chose to attack Iraq in 2003.

Let the Scripture speak for itself:

> And he exerciseth all the power of the first beast before him, and causeth the earth and them which dwell therein to worship the first beast, whose deadly wound was healed. . . . And he had power to give life unto the image of the beast, that the image of the beast should both speak, and cause that as many as would not worship the image of the beast should be killed. And he causeth all, both small and great, rich and poor, free and bond, to receive a mark in their right hand, or in their foreheads. (Revelation 13:12, 15–16)

Many wonder how Jews, Muslims, Buddhists, Hindus, Taoists, Shintoists, animists, skeptics, and atheists could be brought to worship the papacy, but these texts make it plain that the military might of the United States will bring this about.

We greatly admire that evangelist of the early 1950s. He clearly identified only two superpowers at the end of the world—the religio-political power of the papacy and the military-political power of the United States. He therefore declared that the Bible made no room for communism as a major player at the close of this earth's history. Therefore, the mighty power of the Soviet Union, though then appearing as the irresistible force on the planet, here to stay with its communist allies, could not rule the world at the end of earth's history because God's prophetic utterances can never fail.

So impressed were we of this memory of that crusade, that in 1981, Colin began to preach around the world the same message—that the Soviet Union must collapse. He had no idea then that this would become a reality within ten years of when he began to preach this message. In its cover story entitled, "Holy Alliance," *TIME Magazine*, February 24, 1992, detailed the secret alliance of the Vatican with the United States which led to the overthrow of Eastern European communism. The fulfillment of this prophecy of Revelation chapter 13 is rapidly developing at the time of the writing of this book.

Is there today a secret alliance between the Vatican and the United States to effect the same results for the world of Islam? After all, they, too, have to be humbled before this prophecy of Revelation 13 can proceed to complete fulfillment.

If the Bible stood the test for the taming of communism, it will stand the test for the complete fulfilling of the prophecy of Revelation 13. Every obstacle will be overcome by the U.S.-Vatican alliance in its way to enforce obedience to the papacy.

(An in depth study of this prophecy is available in the book *Two Beasts, Three Deadly Wounds, and Fifteen Popes* by the same authors. Available at Hartland Publications.)

CHAPTER 10
Babylon, the City Which Cannot Be Rebuilt

ITS glory days lasted no more than 73 years, yet the city of Babylon has left an enduring legacy which has a significant impact to this day. It conjures up images of ruthless conquest, autocratic rulership, magnificent structures, and a glorious city. Though Babylon (Babel) dates back to early post-diluvian times, having been founded by Nimrod, a great-grandson of Noah, yet it took about 1500 years before Babylon reached its zenith, between 612 B.C. (when Nabopolassar, Nebuchadnezzar's father, destroyed Nineveh) and 539 B.C. (when the city was conquered by the Medo-Persian army). Nebuchadnezzar reigned 44 years, thus most of the 73 glory years of the Babylonian Empire.

After Nebuchadnezzar had comprehensively destroyed Jerusalem in 586 B.C., the Babylonian Empire seemed to be invincible, yet it survived only another 47 years. After the death of Nebuchadnezzar, the kingdom was rapidly weakened by intrigues, assassinations, and short reigns before Nabonidus took the rulership of Babylon. The kingdom was further weakened when Nabonidus took up residence in Taima (or Tayma), Arabia for more than ten years, leaving his son Belshazzar in charge of the day-to-day administration of the kingdom. It was during this time that, when Belshazzar and his lords, rulers, and noblemen were in a drunken state, the Medo-Persians overran this kingdom, and it was never to be reestablished again. However, we are getting ahead of the predictions of the prophets Isaiah and Jeremiah.

First, let us address the circumstances of the Middle East at the time of the overthrow of the Babylonian Empire. The Mediterranean region of the world was one of the most densely populated upon the planet at that time. The major culture of the world was advanced for that time, dominating the Middle East, North Africa with Southern Europe beginning to emerge as a major player. However the heyday of the European nations such as Greece and Rome were centuries away. By the sixth century B.C., Egypt was well past its heyday; therefore, it was almost inevitable that if there were to be a power to overthrow the might of the Babylonians, it would be another Middle East power. Yet no nation had the confidence to attack Babylon on its own.

It will be recalled from your reading of the chapter entitled "A King's Dream" that Babylon, led by King Nabopolassar, had sought an alliance with Cyaxares, king of the Medes, to overthrow and thoroughly destroy Nineveh, the capital of the Assyrian Empire, in 612 B.C. However, there was a decline in the power of Media, and eventually it was defeated by Cyrus, king of Persia. The enlightened Cyrus did not enslave the Medes; rather, he forged a dual kingdom with the Medes, making it feasible to challenge the might of a rapidly weakening Babylonia. It cannot be overlooked that when Babylon was conquered by the Medo-Persians, it was not a Persian king who ruled its new province of Babylonia, but it was Darius, a Mede.

> In that night was Belshazzar the king of the Chaldeans slain. And Darius the Median took the kingdom, being about threescore and two years old. (Daniel 5:30–31)

This passage does not mean that Darius was the supreme king of the Medo-Persian Empire, for Cyrus, a Persian, was the supreme king over the whole of the empire.

Now we turn to the prophecies of Isaiah and Jeremiah. Isaiah prophesied before Babylon reached its glory days, and Jeremiah prophesied when Babylon was undisputed ruler in the eastern, southern, and northern part of the Mediterranean region. Isaiah's prophecy proclaimed in the early part of the seventh century B.C. is especially remarkable. Here are his words:

> And Babylon, the glory of kingdoms, the beauty of the Chaldees' excellency, shall be as when God overthrew

Sodom and Gomorrah. It shall never be inhabited, neither shall it be dwelt in from generation to generation: neither shall the Arabian pitch tent there; neither shall the shepherds make their fold there. But wild beasts of the desert shall lie there; and their houses shall be full of doleful creatures; and owls shall dwell there, and satyrs shall dance there. (Isaiah 13:19–21)

At the time of the writing of this prophecy the main enemy of the Babylonians was Assyria, and the city of Babylon had been destroyed by the Assyrian king, Sennacherib. At this time, the Medes were increasing in military strength but were not a threat to Babylon. The fulfillment of the above prophecy was hundreds of years away. Indeed, for centuries after the overthrow of the kingdom, Babylon still was a prominent city. Its decline becomes evident in the records of history by the early third century B.C. By the time of Christ, most of Babylon was desolate. Yet a Christian church was there in the times of Peter.

> The church that is at Babylon, elected together with you, saluteth you; and so doth Marcus my son. (1 Peter 5:13)

However, by the beginning of the second century A.D., Babylon was wholly desolated without an inhabitant, and it has never been rebuilt.

There is another significant prophecy concerning the destiny of Babylon in the book of Isaiah:

> And, behold, here cometh a chariot of men, with a couple of horsemen. And he answered and said, Babylon is fallen, is fallen; and all the graven images of her gods he hath broken unto the ground. (Isaiah 21:9)

This is the first time the term, "is fallen, is fallen" is used in the Bible concerning Babylon. It is also found in a prophecy applied to ancient Babylon by Jeremiah.

> Babylon is suddenly fallen and destroyed: howl for her; take balm for her pain, if so be she may be healed. (Jeremiah 51:8)

It is also applied to modern "Babylon," the pseudonym for Rome in the New Testament.

> And there followed another angel, saying, Babylon is fallen, is fallen, that great city, because she made all nations drink of the wine of the wrath of her fornication. (Revelation 14:8)

> And he cried mightily with a strong voice, saying, Babylon the great is fallen, is fallen, and is become the habitation of devils, and the hold of every foul spirit, and a cage of every unclean and hateful bird. (Revelation 18:2)

It should be noted that, in spite of the light of the true God received through Daniel and others, Babylon persisted in her idolatry. God's mercy extended long for this city, even until apostolic times, but in the end, God's mercy was withdrawn, and the prophecy of Isaiah was fulfilled until this day.

Now let us review the repeated prophecies of Jeremiah covering the desolation of Babylon. In many verses of prophetic warning its impending doom was uttered and foretold. Below are the main forebodings:

1. Babylon would be like Sodom.

> As God overthrew Sodom and Gomorrah and the neighbour cities thereof, saith the Lord; so shall no man abide there, neither shall any son of man dwell therein. (Jeremiah 50:40)

This comparison with Sodom implied that never again would the city of Babylon be rebuilt, for Sodom has not been rebuilt. (See chapter entitled "Sodom and Gomorrah.")

2. Babylon would be destroyed utterly.

> And the land shall tremble and sorrow: for every purpose of the Lord shall be performed against Babylon, to make the land of Babylon a desolation without an inhabitant. (Jeremiah 51:29)

3. Babylon would remain desolate.

> And Babylon shall become heaps, a dwellingplace for dragons, an astonishment, and an hissing, without an inhabitant. (Jeremiah 51:37)

> Then shalt thou say, O Lord, thou hast spoken against this place, to cut it off, that none shall remain in it, neither man nor beast, but that it shall be desolate for ever. (Jeremiah 51:62)

4. Babylon would be uninhabited.

> And the land shall tremble and sorrow: for every purpose of the Lord shall be performed against Babylon, to make the land of Babylon a desolation without an inhabitant. (Jeremiah 51:29)

However, even more emphatic is the early record of Jeremiah that Babylon would never again be inhabited.

> Therefore the wild beasts of the desert with the wild beasts of the islands shall dwell there, and the owls shall dwell therein: and it shall be no more inhabited for ever; neither shall it be dwelt in from generation to generation. (Jeremiah 50:39)

5. Babylon would become a dry land.

> A drought is upon her waters; and they shall be dried up: for it is the land of graven images, and they are mad upon their idols. (Jeremiah 50:38)

> Her cities are a desolation, a dry land, and a wilderness, a land wherein no man dwelleth, neither doth any son of man pass thereby. (Jeremiah 51:43)

6. The destruction of the city would be sudden.

> Babylon is suddenly fallen and destroyed: howl for her; take balm for her pain, if so be she may be healed. (Jeremiah 51:8)

The attack by the Medo-Persian army was totally unexpected.

7. The city was destroyed because God punished her for her cruelty and wickedness.

> And I will render unto Babylon and to all the inhabitants of Chaldea all their evil that they have done in Zion in your sight, saith the LORD. Behold, I am against thee, O destroying mountain, saith the LORD, which destroyest all the earth: and I will stretch out mine hand upon thee, and roll thee down from the rocks, and will make thee a burnt mountain. (Jeremiah 51:24–25)

8. God used the Medes from the north to destroy Babylon.

> For out of the north there cometh up a nation against her, which shall make her land desolate, and none shall

dwell therein: they shall remove, they shall depart, both man and beast. (Jeremiah 50:3)

Like Isaiah before him, Jeremiah identified that it would be the Medes who would destroy Babylon. The Median kingdom was north of Babylon.

And all the kings of Zimri, and all the kings of Elam, and all the kings of the Medes. (Jeremiah 25:25)

Make bright the arrows; gather the shields: the Lord hath raised up the spirit of the kings of the Medes: for his device is against Babylon, to destroy it; because it is the vengeance of the Lord, the vengeance of his temple. (Jeremiah 51:11)

Prepare against her the nations with the kings of the Medes, the captains thereof, and all the rulers thereof, and all the land of his dominion. (Jeremiah 51:28)

Because it was the Median army which destroyed Babylon, it was only reasonable that Darius, a king of Media, would rule that region of the Medo-Persian Empire. Remember, neither Isaiah nor Jeremiah lived to see this prophecy fulfilled.

So here is a series of detailed prophecies concerning Babylon. They are not unclear details. If any one of these prophecies failed, it would cause great doubt regarding the veracity of biblical prophecy.

Let us review a few of these issues. Added together, these prophecies have had remarkable fulfillment.

1. We will commence with the least remarkable prophecy concerning Babylon—that Babylon would be made desolate (Jeremiah 50:26). We say "least remarkable" because Babylon itself had made two great cities desolate—Nineveh and Jerusalem.

2. However, it was very unlikely that the Medes would destroy Babylon (Isaiah 13:19–21). Especially when Isaiah wrote this

prophecy, the Medes were not distinguished as a powerful military nation.

3. Far more remarkable is the prophecy that this region would become a dry place. Babylon was located close to the delta area of the Red Sea. The Tigris-Euphrates valley was a bountiful, well-watered valley in those days. Indeed, it was the bread basket in that region.

4. However, the most striking fulfillment is that Babylon would never be rebuilt. Let us remind our readers of Jeremiah's claim that Babylon would be desolate *forever*.

> Then shalt thou say, O LORD, thou hast spoken against this place, to cut it off, that none shall remain in it, neither man nor beast, but that it shall be desolate for ever. (Jeremiah 51:62)

It is well beyond 2,500 years since the Medo-Persians conquered Babylon, yet the prophecy of the total desolation of Babylon did not take place until more than 600 years later. How long is the patience and longsuffering of God! It was not until the beginning of the second century A.D., when Emperor Trajan ruled the Roman Empire, that the city of Babylon was fully laid waste.

For 1900 years, the site of Ancient Babylon has defied man to rebuild the city and thus lay claims that the Bible is not the revelation of the all-knowing God of the universe. Indeed, an attempt to prove this was undertaken by a wealthy British atheist in the latter part of the nineteenth century. It was not uncommon for fervent Christians to challenge atheists with the fact that the prophet Jeremiah had prophesied that the city of Babylon would never be rebuilt. This British man had been so challenged, he determined to put an end to such challenges. This man of wealth decided that it would be an exciting project to rebuild such a famous city as close to its original beauty as possible. However, in so doing he would end forever the "hoax" of Christianity. Surprisingly, he was quickly successful in attracting a sizable group of adventuresome artisans to accompany him to the site of ancient Babylon. This large party crossed over Europe to the Middle East, traveling to the location of the site of the Euphrates River. At night, they would pitch tents in which to sleep.

One morning, the leader of the expedition failed to appear at his usual arising time. After some delay, one of the party decided to investigate, and to his horror he found the atheist dead. In great shock, there was much discussion as to what to do. Some wanted to continue and build Babylon as a monument to the "vision" of this atheist. Eventually, more reasoned minds warned that there could well be a curse on this site, and it would be wise to abandon the project. Thus the city remained unbuilt.

Far more well known was Saddam Hussein's determination to rebuild Babylon. What a disastrous decision! The news magazines and major newspapers gave considerable attention to this ambition, which was published in the late 1980s. Colin immediately preached widely around the world that, on the authority of Jeremiah's prophecy, Babylon would not be rebuilt. Colin, of course, did not foresee the 1991 Desert Storm attack on Iraq, nor the 2003 attack on Iraq and the later execution of Saddam, but he had absolute confidence in the biblical record. The barren wastes of ancient Babylon testify of the validity of the words of the Apostle Peter, that God's Word will never fail:

> For all flesh is as grass, and all the glory of man as the flower of grass. The grass withereth, and the flower thereof falleth away: but the word of the Lord endureth for ever. And this is the word which by the gospel is preached unto you. (1 Peter 1:24–25)

We would admonish all who challenge the Word of God that such a challenge can lead to fearful consequences.

Chapter 11
Jerusalem, the Eternal City?

WHAT could have been more improbable than the rebuilding of Jerusalem, the City of David, in the early part of the sixth century B.C. after it had been comprehensively destroyed by three invasions of Nebuchadnezzar, king of Babylon (605, 597, and 586 B.C.)? Most of the destruction took place in 586, when Nebuchadnezzar became enraged by the repeated insurrections in Palestine and decided to put a final end to the kingdom of Judah. This was when most of the Jews were taken captive and placed in servitude in Babylon. However, Daniel, Hananiah, Mishael, and Azariah, the four faithful servants of God, had been taken captive by Nebuchadnezzar's army during his first invasion in 605 B.C. In the third siege, the walls were broken down, the homes were destroyed, and, worst of all, the magnificent center of worship, Solomon's Temple, was totally destroyed. Most of the Jews were carried away into slavery to Babylon. It is true that, in spite of Nebuchadnezzar's reputation as a ruthless and cruel dictator (he burned exiled Jews who were chief agitators in his kingdom), he was also to exhibit levels of enlightenment in his rulership. For example, he trained the wisest of his captives to be princes, governors, captains, judges, treasurers, counselors, sheriffs, and rulers of the provinces.

> Then Nebuchadnezzar the king sent to gather together the princes, the governors, and the captains, the judges, the treasurers, the counsellors, the sheriffs, and all the rulers of the provinces, to come to the dedication of the image which Nebuchadnezzar the king had set up. (Daniel 3:2)

The weeping and wailing of the Jews for their beloved city was great. However, for those who remembered the Scriptures, there was the promise that they would return after seventy years.

> And this whole land shall be a desolation, and an astonishment; and these nations shall serve the king of Babylon seventy years. (Jeremiah 25:11)

Judah had been constantly warned by the prophets over the years. God had sent His loving rebukes, but ultimately God's Word was rejected. Many years before the Babylonian captivity, Isaiah had borne testimony of the terrible spiritual sickness in Judah.

> Ah sinful nation, a people laden with iniquity, a seed of evildoers, children that are corrupters: they have forsaken the LORD, they have provoked the Holy One of Israel unto anger, they are gone away backward. (Isaiah 1:4)

With prophetic utterances Isaiah prophesied what would take place.

> Your country is desolate, your cities are burned with fire: your land, strangers devour it in your presence, and it is desolate, as overthrown by strangers. (Isaiah 1:7)

The Lord had warned that if it had not been for a very small, faithful remnant remaining loyal to Him, Jerusalem would have been obliterated from the face of eternity as had been Sodom and Gomorrah.

> Except the LORD of hosts had left unto us a very small remnant, we should have been as Sodom, and we should have been like unto Gomorrah. (Isaiah 1:9)

You may recall that God would have saved Sodom and Gomorrah if there had been ten faithful men in those cities. (See chapter entitled "Sodom and Gomorrah.") But not even ten men of God could be found.

It is heart-moving to know how patient and longsuffering God is with His people. Many warnings were given through the prophet Jeremiah before Nebuchadnezzar's first military expedition against Jerusalem. Many times, Jeremiah lamented the terrible spiritual treachery of those who were claiming to be God's people.

> Oh that I had in the wilderness a lodging place of wayfaring men; that I might leave my people, and go from them! for they be all adulterers, an assembly of treacherous men. And they bend their tongues like their bow for lies: but they are not valiant for the truth upon the earth; for they proceed from evil to evil, and they know not me, saith the LORD. (Jeremiah 9:2–3)

If a traveler visited Jerusalem and Babylon after the complete destruction of Jerusalem, surely that traveler would have said, "Jerusalem is destroyed forever. This barren plateau on the top of Mount Moriah is desolate." Had that traveler continued to Babylon and witnessed the glory, majesty and power of that city, he would have been tempted to declare, "This city is the eternal city." Yet, as we noted, God said that the city of Babylon would be destroyed, made desolate, become uninhabited, and be a dry land.

Two thousand six hundred years ago, did God have anything to say regarding the future of Judah and Jerusalem? Before we look at the prophetic utterances concerning the reestablishment of Judah, let us read Jeremiah's description of Israel and Judah after the Babylonian invasion.

> Israel is a scattered sheep; the lions have driven him away: first the king of Assyria hath devoured him; and last this Nebuchadrezzar king of Babylon hath broken his bones. (Jeremiah 50:17)

God's people had fallen into such wickedness that God could not protect them against the king of Babylon, yet they were still His people. Jeremiah, the prophet of God, continued with these words:

> Therefore thus saith the LORD of hosts, the God of Israel; Behold, I will punish the king of Babylon and his land, as I have punished the king of Assyria. (Jeremiah 50:18)

At the time this prophecy was made, Nineveh had been utterly destroyed, and Assyria had become a vassal state of Babylon. We have already seen how Babylon, too, was to be made desolate. Yet, in the same prophecy, Jeremiah delivered a wonderful promise from God to the children of Israel who were in captivity.

> They shall be carried to Babylon, and there shall they be until the day that I visit them, saith the LORD; then will I bring them up, and restore them to this place. (Jeremiah 27:22)

> Thus speaketh the LORD God of Israel, saying, Write thee all the words that I have spoken unto thee in a book. For, lo, the days come, saith the LORD, that I will bring again the captivity of my people Israel and Judah, saith the LORD: and I will cause them to return to the land that I gave to their fathers, and they shall possess it. (Jeremiah 30:2–3)

> And I will bring Israel again to his habitation, and he shall feed on Carmel and Bashan, and his soul shall be satisfied upon mount Ephraim and Gilead. (Jeremiah 50:19)

This is the assurance that the desolate city of Jerusalem in the land of Judah would be reestablished and God's people would have the opportunity to return to their homeland. God did not give this message only once; He gave it many times. Let us look at the final promise in the book of the prophet Amos.

> And I will bring again the captivity of my people of Israel, and they shall build the waste cities, and inhabit

them; and they shall plant vineyards, and drink the wine thereof; they shall also make gardens, and eat the fruit of them. And I will plant them upon their land, and they shall no more be pulled up out of their land which I have given them, saith the LORD thy God. (Amos 9:14–15)

Once again, however, it is Jeremiah who repeatedly assured God's people that they would be reestablished and would rebuild their city and nation. Let us review a number of these texts:

> And I will be found of you, saith the LORD: and I will turn away your captivity, and I will gather you from all the nations, and from all the places whither I have driven you, saith the LORD; and I will bring you again into the place whence I caused you to be carried away captive. (Jeremiah 29:14)

> For, lo, the days come, saith the LORD, that I will bring again the captivity of my people Israel and Judah, saith the LORD: and I will cause them to return to the land that I gave to their fathers, and they shall possess it. (Jeremiah 30:3)

> Thus saith the LORD; Behold, I will bring again the captivity of Jacob's tents, and have mercy on his dwellingplaces; and the city shall be builded upon her own heap, and the palace shall remain after the manner thereof. (Jeremiah 30:18)

> Call unto me, and I will answer thee, and shew thee great and mighty things, which thou knowest not. (Jeremiah 33:3)

Nevertheless, in spite of the promise to restore them to their habitation, God warned that it would be necessary for His people to endure a time of punishment for their rebellion:

> For, lo, I begin to bring evil on the city which is called by my name, and should ye be utterly unpunished? Ye shall not be unpunished: for I will call for a sword upon all the inhabitants of the earth, saith the LORD of hosts. (Jeremiah 25:29)

Two other texts indicated that God would not make a full end of the Jewish people.

> For thus hath the LORD said, The whole land shall be desolate; yet will I not make a full end. (Jeremiah 4:27)

> And I will bring Israel again to his habitation, and he shall feed on Carmel and Bashan, and his soul shall be satisfied upon mount Ephraim and Gilead. (Jeremiah 50:19)

In conjunction with the promise that He would not make a full end of Judah, nevertheless, by contrast, God foretells that He would make a full end of other nations.

> For I am with thee, saith the LORD, to save thee: though I make a full end of all nations whither I have scattered thee, yet will I not make a full end of thee: but I will correct thee in measure, and will not leave thee altogether unpunished. (Jeremiah 30:11)

Once again, the people of God would not go unpunished; nevertheless, God would not make a full end of them.

> And I will render unto Babylon and to all the inhabitants of Chaldea all their evil that they have done in Zion in your sight, saith the LORD. (Jeremiah 51:24)

Perhaps the most comprehensive promise which God made through Jeremiah is to be found in chapter 46:

> But fear not thou, O my servant Jacob, and be not dismayed, O Israel: for, behold, I will save thee from afar off, and thy seed from the land of their captivity; and Jacob shall return, and be in rest and at ease, and none shall make him afraid. Fear thou not, O Jacob my servant, saith the LORD: for I am with thee; for I will make a full end of all the nations whither I have driven thee: but I will not make a full end of thee, but correct thee in measure; yet will I not leave thee wholly unpunished. (Jeremiah 46:27–28)

Many of the nations which surrounded Israel are no longer in existence—the Philistines, Moabites, Ammonites, Edomites, Hittites, and the Jebusites, to name just a few—but Israel remains today.

As we will see in the chapter entitled "The Years of Christ's Ministry and Sacrifice Foretold," God had set aside a 490-year period of time for His people, and it was not until some years after that time ended that Jerusalem suffered a destruction that was never to be followed by a divine blessing—whether or not the city would be rebuilt.

Whether or not the nation of Israel and the city of Jerusalem have a role in end-time prophecy is a question outside the scope of this book. However, it remains a fact that the city of Jerusalem has been rebuilt more than once since Nebuchadnezzar destroyed it, and it is still, though a troubled city, strong and prosperous as we have witnessed. This prophecy is remarkable in that at the time of the Babylonian captivity the people of Judah had forsaken God except for a very small remnant. Yet God did not forsake them.

> For Israel hath not been forsaken, nor Judah of his God, of the LORD of hosts; though their land was filled with sin against the Holy One of Israel. (Jeremiah 51:5)

Thus we see the contrast of two prominent cities which existed well over twenty-five hundred years ago. Because of their insubordination, the Jews suffered fearfully, yet God did not leave them nor forsake them during almost one thousand years since their captivity in Egypt.

The glorious city of Babylon, the might of the Babylonian Empire, was to fail, and that city would never be built again. It would be laid waste, and never again in the history of this world would the city of Babylon be rebuilt.

How remarkable and enduring are those prophecies of the Bible, for they are fulfilled with pinpoint accuracy! Today, Jerusalem is a most significant city in the world. Babylon is not. It is a living testimony to the enduring, unfailing Word of God. How can the skeptics challenge these prophecies which have endured the tests over millennia of subsequent history? We surely can trust the ancient prophesies of the Word of God.

Of course, the city of Jerusalem will not last forever, for, like all human structures, it will be consumed when God destroys this earth by fire. However, the New Jerusalem built by God will undoubtedly exist eternally.

CHAPTER 12
Messianic Prophecies of Christ's Birth and Ministry

THE Old Testament is replete with many specific details concerning the coming Messiah. Some of these prophecies will be familiar to readers who have been blessed by the rendition of Handel's oratorio *The Messiah*. These readers will recognize these texts when we explain them in this chapter. A number of Messianic prophecies are to be found in both the earlier and later writings of the prophet Isaiah—more than most other prophets. The Psalms are another rich source of Messianic prophecy as well as are some of the so-called minor prophets.

Some readers, no doubt, will protest that the writers of the New Testament were very familiar with the Old Testament prophecies, so what guarantee do we have that they did not insert into their gospels unsubstantiated materials, claiming they were fulfillments of these prophecies when such events had not taken place? There will always be those who will deny the truths of history.

For example, a significant group of individuals deny the Holocaust of the Jews. Colin has been to Auschwitz in Poland and Dachau in Germany. Did the Jews build these camps so as to deceive the world? Of course not. In the 1950s, Colin taught for more than three and one half years at *Mount Moriah War Memorial College*, a primary (elementary) school operated by Orthodox Jews in Sydney, Australia. Were the tattooed numbers on the upper arms of these Jews, as they claimed, the evidence that they had been prisoners in concentration camps? Colin is a believer that they did indeed suffer in these terrible camps.

Messianic Prophecies of Christ's Birth and Ministry

For some people, no amount of object evidence will convince them of the veracity of Christ's atoning sacrifice for the human race. This book is written for honest seekers after truth who are earnestly looking for and desire to accept the objective evidence of Christ who is the Redeemer of the world. This chapter deals with the birth and earthly ministry of Christ.

There are more than sixty prophecies concerning the birth, ministry, and death of Jesus Christ in the Old Testament. If there were any questions about the authenticity of the Old Testament, they were dispelled by the discovery of the Dead Sea Scrolls in the middle of the twentieth century. These scrolls antedate the birth of Christ. At least significant fragments of 38 of the 39 Old Testament books were discovered. Only the book of Esther was missing. Some were nearly complete, and the scroll of Isaiah was complete, thus verifying the accuracy of the best modern Old Testament translations.

We will not address all the prophecies but will point to a sample of these prophecies.

1. The Old Testament prophesied that Christ's human heritage would be of the Tribe of Judah, a descendent of King David:

> The sceptre shall not depart from Judah, nor a lawgiver from between his feet, until Shiloh come; and unto him shall the gathering of the people be. (Genesis 49:10)

> And in that day there shall be a root of Jesse, which shall stand for an ensign of the people; to it shall the Gentiles seek: and his rest shall be glorious. (Isaiah 11:10)

King David was the son of Jesse, of the tribe of Judah.

Mathew and Luke both trace Christ's human genealogy to the tribe of Judah.

> The book of the generation of Jesus Christ, the son of David, the son of Abraham. Abraham begat Isaac; and Isaac begat Jacob; and Jacob begat Judas and his brethren; and Judas begat Phares and Zara of Thamar; and Phares

begat Esrom; and Esrom begat Aram. . . . And Jacob begat Joseph the husband of Mary, of whom was born Jesus, who is called Christ. (Matthew 1:1–3, 16)

Note that though Joseph the husband of Mary was not Jesus' genetic father, he, like Mary, was of the tribe of Judah as recorded in the genealogy of Luke, which was given in reverse order. (See Luke 3:23–33.) It will be noted that both genealogies go back beyond the generation of David, the second king of Israel and a descendent from Judah, the third son of Jacob.

2. Though of the tribe of Judah, the Messiah would grow up in and minister in Galilee in the north, which was separated from the land of Judah with Samaria located between.

> Nevertheless the dimness shall not be such as was in her vexation, when at the first he lightly afflicted the land of Zebulun and the land of Naphtali, and afterward did more grievously afflict her by the way of the sea, beyond Jordan, in Galilee of the nations. The people that walked in darkness have seen a great light: they that dwell in the land of the shadow of death, upon them hath the light shined. (Isaiah 9:1–2)

This is confirmed in the New Testament.

> And leaving Nazareth, he came and dwelt in Capernaum, which is upon the sea coast, in the borders of Zabulon and Nephthalim: that it might be fulfilled which was spoken by Esaias the prophet, saying, the land of Zabulon, and the land of Nephthalim, by the way of the sea, beyond Jordan, Galilee of the Gentiles; the people which sat in darkness saw great light; and to them which sat in the region and shadow of death light is sprung up. (Matthew 4:13–16)

3. Amazingly, though Joseph and Mary lived in Galilee, it was prophesied by Micah that Jesus would be born in Bethlehem, a small city of Judah.

> But thou, Bethlehem Ephratah, though thou be little among the thousands of Judah, yet out of thee shall he come forth unto me that is to be ruler in Israel; whose goings forth have been from of old, from everlasting. (Micah 5:2)

This came about when Caesar Augustus decreed that all the Jews be taxed. Because Joseph was of the house of David, he was required to go to the City of David—Bethlehem—to be taxed, and there Jesus was born.

> And it came to pass in those days, that there went out a decree from Caesar Augustus, that all the world should be taxed. (And this taxing was first made when Cyrenius was governor of Syria.) And all went to be taxed, every one into his own city. And Joseph also went up from Galilee, out of the city of Nazareth, into Judaea, unto the city of David, which is called Bethlehem; (because he was of the house and lineage of David:) to be taxed with Mary his espoused wife, being great with child. And so it was, that, while they were there, the days were accomplished that she should be delivered. And she brought forth her firstborn son, and wrapped him in swaddling clothes, and laid him in a manger; because there was no room for them in the inn. . . . For unto you is born this day in the city of David a Saviour, which is Christ the Lord. (Luke 2:1–7, 11)

4. The prophet Isaiah foretold that Jesus would be conceived in the womb of a virgin.

> Therefore the Lord himself shall give you a sign; Behold, a virgin shall conceive, and bear a son, and shall call his name Immanuel. (Isaiah 7:14)

This was miraculously fulfilled as the New Testament explains.

> And the angel said unto her, Fear not, Mary: for thou hast found favour with God. . . . Then said Mary unto the angel, How shall this be, seeing I know not a man? And the angel answered and said unto her, The Holy Ghost shall come upon thee, and the power of the Highest shall overshadow thee: therefore also that holy thing which shall be born of thee shall be called the Son of God. (Luke 1:30, 34–35)

> Behold, a virgin shall be with child, and shall bring forth a son, and they shall call his name Emmanuel, which being interpreted is, God with us. (Matthew 1:23)

This virgin birth is one of the greatest stumbling blocks for atheists. Some, for example, correctly have discovered that the Hebrew word *almah* can be not only translated "virgin" but also "maid" or "maiden." This is also true of *parthos*, the Greek word translated "virgin." However, we must understand that the term *maiden* meant a young woman who had not had sexual intercourse. Even in the English-speaking world, the first sexual intercourse of a woman is often referred to as "to break her maiden." In other words, she is no longer a virgin. While this miraculous virgin birth is a mystery to humanity, it is fully understood by God.

5. The Old Testament also prophesied the terrible slaughter of babies soon after the birth of Jesus.

> Thus saith the LORD; A voice was heard in Ramah, lamentation, and bitter weeping; Rahel weeping for her

children refused to be comforted for her children, because they were not. (Jeremiah 31:15)

Here is the very sad fulfillment of this prophecy.

> Then Herod, when he saw that he was mocked of the wise men, was exceeding wroth, and sent forth, and slew all the children that were in Bethlehem, and in all the coasts thereof, from two years old and under, according to the time which he had diligently enquired of the wise men. Then was fulfilled that which was spoken by Jeremy the prophet, saying, In Rama was there a voice heard, lamentation, and weeping, and great mourning, Rachel weeping for her children, and would not be comforted, because they are not. (Matthew 2:16–18)

How was it that Jesus was not killed with the other babies? The Bible explains this, too, beginning with the wise men being warned not to return to Herod and tell him the whereabouts of the baby.

> And being warned of God in a dream that they should not return to Herod, they departed into their own country another way. And when they were departed, behold, the angel of the Lord appeareth to Joseph in a dream, saying, Arise, and take the young child and his mother, and flee into Egypt, and be thou there until I bring thee word: for Herod will seek the young child to destroy him. (Matthew 2:12–13)

6. The hasty journey to Egypt had also been prophesied in the Old Testament.

> When Israel was a child, then I loved him, and called my son out of Egypt. (Hosea 11:1)

The fulfillment is faithfully recorded in the gospel of Matthew.

> When he arose, he took the young child and his mother by night, and departed into Egypt: and was there until the death of Herod: that it might be fulfilled which was spoken of the Lord by the prophet, saying, Out of Egypt have I called my son. (Matthew 2:14–15)

7. God declared the messiahship of the baby Jesus to elderly prophets living at that time—the prophet Simeon and the prophetess Anna. No doubt, both had carefully studied the prophecies concerning Christ in the Old Testament.

> And, behold, there was a man in Jerusalem, whose name was Simeon; and the same man was just and devout, waiting for the consolation of Israel: and the Holy Ghost was upon him. And it was revealed unto him by the Holy Ghost, that he should not see death, before he had seen the Lord's Christ. And he came by the Spirit into the temple: and when the parents brought in the child Jesus, to do for him after the custom of the law, then took he him up in his arms, and blessed God, and said, Lord, now lettest thou thy servant depart in peace, according to thy word: for mine eyes have seen thy salvation, which thou hast prepared before the face of all people; a light to lighten the Gentiles, and the glory of thy people Israel. And Joseph and his mother marvelled at those things which were spoken of him. And Simeon blessed them, and said unto Mary his mother, Behold, this child is set for the fall and rising again of many in Israel; and for a sign which shall be spoken against. (Luke 2:25–34)

> And there was one Anna, a prophetess, the daughter of Phanuel, of the tribe of Aser: she was of a great age, and

had lived with an husband seven years from her virginity; and she was a widow of about fourscore and four years, which departed not from the temple, but served God with fastings and prayers night and day. And she coming in that instant gave thanks likewise unto the Lord, and spake of him to all them that looked for redemption in Jerusalem. (Luke 2:36–38)

8. The Old Testament declared that there would be a prophet to proclaim Christ's coming.

> The voice of him that crieth in the wilderness, Prepare ye the way of the Lord, make straight in the desert a highway for our God. Every valley shall be exalted, and every mountain and hill shall be made low: and the crooked shall be made straight, and the rough places plain: and the glory of the Lord shall be revealed, and all flesh shall see it together: for the mouth of the Lord hath spoken it. (Isaiah 40:3–5)

John the Baptist fulfilled that role.

> In those days came John the Baptist, preaching in the wilderness of Judaea, and saying, Repent ye: for the kingdom of heaven is at hand. For this is he that was spoken of by the prophet Esaias, saying, The voice of one crying in the wilderness, Prepare ye the way of the Lord, make his paths straight. (Matthew 3:1–3)

9. We refer to the prophecy of the specific year of the commencement of Christ's ministry in A.D. 27 (see our chapter entitled "The Years of Christ's Ministry and Sacrifice Foretold").

Apart from this, there are few prophecies regarding the detailing His ministry. Most of the Old Testament prophecies focus either upon the details of His birth and early life or upon the events which lead up to His trial and crucifixion. However, there are at least two other events which were foretold.

10. Christ's cleansing of the temple was foretold.

> Even them will I bring to my holy mountain, and make them joyful in my house of prayer: their burnt offerings and their sacrifices shall be accepted upon mine altar; for mine house shall be called an house of prayer for all people. (Isaiah 56:7)

> Is this house, which is called by my name, become a den of robbers in your eyes? Behold, even I have seen it, saith the LORD. (Jeremiah 7:11)

Twice Jesus fulfilled this prophecy—once at the beginning of His ministry and once near the end:

> And Jesus went into the temple of God, and cast out all them that sold and bought in the temple, and overthrew the tables of the moneychangers, and the seats of them that sold doves, And said unto them, It is written, My house shall be called the house of prayer; but ye have made it a den of thieves. (Matthew 21:12–13)

11. Christ's triumphal journey into Jerusalem just before His arrest was also faithfully predicted in the Old Testament.

> Rejoice greatly, O daughter of Zion; shout, O daughter of Jerusalem: behold, thy King cometh unto thee: he is just, and having salvation; lowly, and riding upon an ass, and upon a colt the foal of an ass. (Zechariah 9:9)

Below is the record of the fulfillment of this prophecy.

> And they brought the colt to Jesus, and cast their garments on him; and he sat upon him. And many spread their garments in the way: and others cut down branches off the trees, and strawed them in the way. And they that went before, and they that followed, cried, saying, Hosanna; Blessed is he that cometh in the name of the Lord: blessed be the kingdom of our father David, that cometh in the name of the Lord: Hosanna in the highest. And Jesus entered into Jerusalem, and into the temple: and when he had looked round about upon all things, and now the eventide was come, he went out unto Bethany with the twelve. (Mark 11:7–11)

Some may rationalize that the authors of the gospels went out of their way to fabricate the "evidence" to fit the prophecies. This would be a shallow conclusion. First, it was more than one of the gospel writers who provided the evidence, indicating that no writer systematically attempted such fabrication. Secondly, the gospels of Matthew, Mark, and Luke were all written when large numbers of Jews were still alive who could have been conversant especially with the latter part of Christ's earthly life, and surely, if the writers had fabricated details, there would have been much evidence presented by these people to show that the biblical records were wrong. We have the evidence that Nicodemus and Joseph of Arimathaea, both members of the Sanhedrin, embraced Christ as their Savior—a sure sign that they affirmed the evidence.

> And after this Joseph of Arimathaea, being a disciple of Jesus, but secretly for fear of the Jews, besought Pilate that he might take away the body of Jesus: and Pilate gave him leave. He came therefore, and took the body of Jesus. And there came also Nicodemus, which at the first came to Jesus by night, and brought a mixture of myrrh and aloes, about an hundred pound weight. Then took they the body

> of Jesus, and wound it in linen clothes with the spices, as the manner of the Jews is to bury. Now in the place where he was crucified there was a garden; and in the garden a new sepulchre, wherein was never man yet laid. There laid they Jesus therefore because of the Jews' preparation day; for the sepulchre was nigh at hand. (John 19:38-42)

Remember also that after Christ's death, resurrection, and ascension many embraced the gospel of Jesus.

> And the word of God increased; and the number of the disciples multiplied in Jerusalem greatly; and a great company of the priests were obedient to the faith. (Acts 6:7)

We submit that this collection of messianic prophecies is powerful evidence that the infinite God of the universe is responsible for the prophecies of the Old Testament which were fulfilled in the birth, childhood, and ministry of Jesus.

Chapter 13
The Years of Christ's Ministry and Sacrifice Foretold

PERHAPS our readers will think that there is no end to the remarkable prophecies provided by God through the prophet Daniel. There is an end, of course, but the Old Testament prophet Daniel ranks with John in the New Testament as among the greatest prophets who communicated God's revelations to the human race of events subsequent to their earthly lives. Thus we introduce to you yet another incredible prophecy which God reveals to all who are wise enough to study them. Let us remind you of what Scripture says about the "secrets" of God.

> He revealeth the deep and secret things: he knoweth what is in the darkness, and the light dwelleth with him. (Daniel 2:22)

> We have also a more sure word of prophecy; whereunto ye do well that ye take heed, as unto a light that shineth in a dark place, until the day dawn, and the day star arise in your hearts: knowing this first, that no prophecy of the scripture is of any private interpretation. For the prophecy came not in old time by the will of man: but holy men of God spake as they were moved by the Holy Ghost. (2 Peter 1:19–21)

In the ninth chapter of Daniel there is a prophecy which defies all speculations and ambiguity because of its precise detail concerning the ministry and sacrifice of Christ on Calvary. It actually pinpoints the year

Christ was to be baptized and begin His ministry on earth at 30 years of age and when He would be put to death.

There is an unbroken principle in the prophecies of Daniel and John the Revelator which we have not addressed previously in this book, though this principle applied to all the three prophecies which we have explained from Daniel chapters 2, 7, and 8. This principle is that when numbers are presented they are always literal, but they are also always associated with a symbol. Let us briefly explain a few examples.

1. Daniel 2:42

> And as the toes of the feet were part of iron, and part of clay, so the kingdom shall be partly strong, and partly broken. (Daniel 2:42)

The (ten) toes are representative of the ten kingdoms into which the Roman Empire divided. The number ten represents a literal number, but toes are symbolic of kingdoms. For more details review again the exposition of this prophecy in the chapter of this book entitled, "A King's Dream."

2. Daniel 7:24

> And the ten horns out of this kingdom are ten kings [kingdoms] that shall arise: and another shall rise after them; and he shall be diverse from the first, and he shall subdue three kings [kingdoms]. (Daniel 7:24)

Here again, the numbers were literal, but the horns were symbolic of nations. For more details review again the chapter entitled, "Four Beasts, Ten Horns, and a Little Horn."

3. Daniel 8:3, 5, 8

> Then I lifted up mine eyes, and saw, and, behold, there stood before the river a ram which had two horns: and the

> two horns were high; but one was higher than the other, and the higher came up last.... And as I was considering, behold, an he goat came from the west on the face of the whole earth, and touched not the ground: and the goat had a notable horn between his eyes.... Therefore the he goat waxed very great: and when he was strong, the great horn was broken; and for it came up four notable ones toward the four winds of heaven. (Daniel 8:3, 5, 8)

In this chapter the ten, two, and four were all literal numbers, but they were each associated with a symbol. For more details review the chapter entitled "A Ram and a He Goat."

In the prophecy of Daniel 9, which will now be examined, we see the numbers associated with "weeks." They cannot be literal weeks, for prophetic numbers are always associated in the books of Daniel and Revelation with symbols. We also explored this principle in the chapter entitled, "The Years of Christ's Ministry and Sacrifice Foretold." We learned that days in a prophetic setting are symbolic of years. Here are the two verses of Scripture which support this principle.

> After the number of the days in which ye searched the land, even forty days, each day for a year, shall ye bear your iniquities, even forty years, and ye shall know my breach of promise. (Numbers 14:34)

> And when thou hast accomplished them, lie again on thy right side, and thou shalt bear the iniquity of the house of Judah forty days: I have appointed thee each day for a year. (Ezekiel 4:6)

Now, with the backdrop of these consistent prophetic principles of interpretation, let us focus on the prophecy of Daniel 9.

> Yea, whiles I was speaking in prayer, even the man Gabriel, whom I had seen in the vision at the beginning,

being caused to fly swiftly, touched me about the time of the evening oblation. And he informed me, and talked with me, and said, O Daniel, I am now come forth to give thee skill and understanding. At the beginning of thy supplications the commandment came forth, and I am come to shew thee; for thou art greatly beloved: therefore understand the matter, and consider the vision. Seventy weeks are determined upon thy people and upon thy holy city, to finish the transgression, and to make an end of sins, and to make reconciliation for iniquity, and to bring in everlasting righteousness, and to seal up the vision and prophecy, and to anoint the most Holy. Know therefore and understand, that from the going forth of the commandment to restore and to build Jerusalem unto the Messiah the Prince shall be seven weeks, and threescore and two weeks: the street shall be built again, and the wall, even in troublous times. And after threescore and two weeks shall Messiah be cut off, but not for himself: and the people of the prince that shall come shall destroy the city and the sanctuary; and the end thereof shall be with a flood, and unto the end of the war desolations are determined. And he shall confirm the covenant with many for one week: and in the midst of the week he shall cause the sacrifice and the oblation to cease, and for the overspreading of abominations he shall make it desolate, even until the consummation, and that determined shall be poured upon the desolate. (Daniel 9:21–27)

To many, this short prophecy seems very complicated at first, so we will do our best to explain its meaning. When we translate the weeks into days the understanding of this prophecy is simplified. Thus, 70 weeks becomes 490 days; 7 weeks represents 49 days; three score and two weeks (62 weeks) becomes 434 days; one week, 7 days. Now we remind you that days in prophecy are symbolic of years. Thus the overall prophecy spans a period of exactly 490 years.

Now we must determine the year when this 490-year prophecy began before we can discover not only when it ends but when the other events take place within the 490-year period. The man (angel) Gabriel clarifies the beginning point of this prophecy.

> Know therefore and understand, that from the going forth of the commandment to restore and to build Jerusalem unto the Messiah the Prince shall be seven weeks, and threescore and two weeks: the street shall be built again, and the wall, even in troublous times. (Daniel 9:25)

Note the precision of when this prophecy begins: "from the going forth of the commandment to restore and to [re]build Jerusalem." A search of biblical history leads us to the beginning of this prophecy. The prophet Ezra, the Jewish scribe, provides the information regarding this decree. It is significant that it took the decrees of three kings to fulfill the prophecy of Daniel 9:25.

> And the elders of the Jews builded, and they prospered through the prophesying of Haggai the prophet and Zechariah the son of Iddo. And they builded, and finished it, according to the commandment of the God of Israel, and according to the commandment of Cyrus, and Darius, and Artaxerxes king of Persia. (Ezra 6:14)

Note that Ezra refers to only one commandment (decree), though all three kings made decrees. He refers to the commandment of the three kings in the singular, providing compelling evidence that it required the efforts of the three kings before the decree was completely fulfilled. Ezra gives further detail of when the third king, Artaxerxes, made this decree:

> And there went up some of the children of Israel, and of the priests, and the Levites, and the singers, and the porters, and the Nethinims, unto Jerusalem, in the seventh year of Artaxerxes the king. (Ezra 7:7)

While there were three kings of Persia named Artaxerxes, many historians and scholars believe that this decree was made by Artaxerxes I (Artaxerxes Longimanus), for he reigned at the time when Ezra is believed to have returned to Jerusalem. Evidence seems to indicate most strongly that Ezra, the Jewish scribe, used the Jewish "accession year" system of reckoning, in which they began their civil calendar in the fall, and the calendar year in which a new king began to reign was the "accession year," or we might say, "year zero." According to this system, the first regnal year of the king's reign began with the civil New Year's Day following his accession year. Since Artaxerxes came to the throne in the Jewish year 465–464 B.C., his "first year" began in the fall of 464 B.C., and his seventh regnal year was from the fall of 458 B.C. to the fall of 457 B.C. A number of Old Testament scholars, including seminary professor Dr. William Shea, have provided compelling evidence for this date. Thus we can now begin to extrapolate the dates which end the different times indicated.

Let us begin with the 70 weeks (490 symbolic days / literal years). It is essential to keep in mind that there is no zero year between 1 B.C. and 1 A.D. Thus, instead of 490 years ending in 33 A.D., they end in 34 A.D. when we add 490 years to 457 B.C. What was to happen during these 490 years which ended in 34 A.D.? Here is the answer:

> Seventy weeks are determined upon thy people and upon thy holy city, to finish the transgression, and to make an end of sins, and to make reconciliation for iniquity, and to bring in everlasting righteousness, and to seal up the vision and prophecy, and to anoint the most Holy. (Daniel 9:24)

God, through the prophet Daniel, warned Judah (His chosen people) that He was providing another 490 years to put away sin from the nation. Clearly God gave His chosen people another 490 years to fulfill their chosen role as the ambassadors of the truth of God to the world. The best conclusion we can make is that if the Jews did not return to the Lord and fulfill their holy calling, they would no longer be God's special people. We will address this later in the chapter.

With even more specificity we learn that the seven weeks and three score and two weeks (a total of 69 weeks, or 483 symbolic days / literal years) beginning in 457 B.C. takes us to 27 A.D. Because the decree of Artaxerxes I went into effect in the latter part of 457 B.C., 483 years later brings us to the autumn of 27 A.D., when Jesus was baptized by John the Baptist in the river Jordan. This began Jesus' public teaching, healing, and ministry.

> Then cometh Jesus from Galilee to Jordan unto John, to be baptized of him. But John forbad him, saying, I have need to be baptized of thee, and comest thou to me? And Jesus answering said unto him, Suffer it to be so now: for thus it becometh us to fulfil all righteousness. Then he suffered him. And Jesus, when he was baptized, went up straightway out of the water: and, lo, the heavens were opened unto him, and he saw the Spirit of God descending like a dove, and lighting upon him: and lo a voice from heaven, saying, This is my beloved Son, in whom I am well pleased. (Matthew 3:13–17)

> That word, I say, ye know, which was published throughout all Judaea, and began from Galilee, after the baptism which John preached; how God anointed Jesus of Nazareth with the Holy Ghost and with power: who went about doing good, and healing all that were oppressed of the devil; for God was with him. (Acts 10:37–38)

Jesus knew that this aspect of the time prophecy had now been fulfilled, for after His baptism He declared,

> The time is fulfilled, and the kingdom of God is at hand.... (Mark 1:15)

Now another detail is revealed in Daniel 9:26:

> And *after threescore and two weeks shall Messiah be cut off,* but not for himself: and the people of the prince that shall come shall destroy the city and the sanctuary; and the end thereof shall be with a flood, and unto the end of the war desolations are determined. (Daniel 9:26)

Daniel here records, in another plain reference to Jesus, that He would "be cut off." One of the meanings of the Hebrew word translated "cut off" is to be "destroyed" or to "perish." For example, in Genesis 9:11, the same words "cut off" are used to imply the deaths of the antediluvians at the time of Noah's flood.

> And I will establish my covenant with you; neither shall all flesh be cut off any more by the waters of a flood; neither shall there any more be a flood to destroy the earth. (Genesis 9:11)

This prophecy reaches farther in verse 27 with the precise time when Jesus would die for the sins of the human race.

> And he shall confirm the covenant with many for one week: and *in the midst of the week* he shall cause the sacrifice and the oblation to cease, and for the overspreading of abominations he shall make it desolate, even until the consummation, and that determined shall be poured upon the desolate. (Daniel 9:27)

Note that Jesus would die "in the midst of the week," half way through the seven-year period after the beginning of His ministry—that is, after a period of three and a half years (half of seven years). This would indicate that Christ would die in the spring of A.D. 31. The Scriptures confirm that the Sabbath during which Jesus was resting in the tomb was not any ordinary Sabbath; it was a "high" Sabbath, for it was also the time of the Passover, which occurred in the spring.

> And it was the preparation of the passover, and about the sixth hour: and he saith unto the Jews, Behold your King! But they cried out, Away with him, away with him, crucify him. Pilate saith unto them, Shall I crucify your King? The chief priests answered, We have no king but Caesar. Then delivered he him therefore unto them to be crucified. And they took Jesus, and led him away. (John 19:14–16)

> The Jews therefore, because it was the preparation, that the bodies should not remain upon the cross on the sabbath day, (for that sabbath day was an high day,) besought Pilate that their legs might be broken, and that they might be taken away. (John 19:31)

How amazing is the fulfillment of this prophecy!

However, there is another detail to address. Remember that the Jews were given 70 weeks (490 years) "to finish the transgression, and to make an end of sins. . . ." (Daniel 9:24) Sadly, they did not, during this 490-year period, bring an end to transgression and sin; neither did they, as a nation, receive Jesus as their Savior and Redeemer. There is Scriptural evidence that it was the rejection of Christ, finalized in the decision to crucify Him, that ended the Jewish nation's status as God's favored people.

After Jesus raised Lazarus from the dead, the priests and Pharisees counseled together and decided to take steps to put Jesus to death, and there was nothing more that could be done by God to reach this people as a nation. Not long after, when Jesus made His triumphal entry into Jerusalem, He surprised everyone at the brow of Olivet, overlooking the city:

> And when he was come near, he beheld the city, and wept over it, saying, If thou hadst known, even thou, at least in this thy day, the things which belong unto thy peace! but now they are hid from thine eyes. For the days shall come upon thee, that thine enemies shall cast a trench about thee, and compass thee round, and keep thee in on

every side, and shall lay thee even with the ground, and thy children within thee; and they shall not leave in thee one stone upon another; because thou knewest not the time of thy visitation. (Luke 19:41–44)

Here Jesus foretold the nation's punishment that would be fulfilled thirty-plus years after His crucifixion.

As we review again verse 26 of Daniel 9, we will note that the prophecy declares that the city and the sanctuary would be destroyed.

And after threescore and two weeks shall Messiah be cut off, but not for himself: and *the people of the prince that shall come shall destroy the city and the sanctuary*; and the end thereof shall be with a flood, and unto the end of the war desolations are determined. (Daniel 9:26)

This prophecy was fulfilled in 70 A.D., when the Roman army under Titus, its commander-in-chief, desolated the city of Jerusalem and destroyed the beautiful temple which was so revered by the Jews. This destruction of the city of Jerusalem and its temple is faithfully recorded by historians:

In 66 [A.D.] the Jews rebelled against Rome, and in 70 the city was besieged and almost wholly destroyed by the Roman forces under the future emperor Titus. The Temple, Herod's greatest achievement, was reduced to ashes. ("Jerusalem." *Encyclopaedia Britannica 2007 Ultimate Reference Suite*)

Yet this destruction was not the end of the city of Jerusalem. (See chapter entitled, "Jerusalem, the Eternal City?")

That the Jewish nation's doom resulted from their final rejection of Christ was also reflected in Jesus' cursing of the fig tree, which symbolized the nation (see Matthew 21:17–19), and His pronouncement as He left the temple for the last time:

> O Jerusalem, Jerusalem, thou that killest the prophets, and stonest them which are sent unto thee, how often would I have gathered thy children together, even as a hen gathereth her chickens under her wings, and ye would not! Behold, your house is left unto you desolate. (Matthew 23:37–38)

> And Jesus went out, and departed from the temple: and his disciples came to him for to shew him the buildings of the temple. And Jesus said unto them, See ye not all these things? verily I say unto you, There shall not be left here one stone upon another, that shall not be thrown down. (Matthew 24:1–2)

From this time on, the Jewish nation would no longer be God's chosen people, yet they still had an opportunity, as individuals, to be part of the kingdom of Christ. There were many individual Jews who were secret followers of Christ. And there were many others who had been deceived by the Jewish leaders. Therefore, God, in His mercy, provided three and a half years after the crucifixion of Jesus for the gospel to be directed especially to the Jews, that they might be given the first chance to accept the Messiahship of Jesus with the abundance of evidence available of His death, resurrection, and ascension back to heaven.

> But ye shall receive power, after that the Holy Ghost is come upon you: and ye shall be witnesses unto me both in Jerusalem, and in all Judaea, and in Samaria, and unto the uttermost part of the earth. (Acts 1:8)

In this three-and-a-half-year period after the death of Jesus, thousands responded to the gospel message, as is recorded in the book of Acts.

> Howbeit many of them which heard the word believed; and the number of the men was about five thousand. (Acts 4:4)

> And the word of God increased; and the number of the disciples multiplied in Jerusalem greatly; and a great company of the priests were obedient to the faith. (Acts 6:7)

However, as a nation, the large majority of the Jewish leaders and people rejected their Messiah and persecuted the Jews who embraced Christianity.

> ... And at that time there was a great persecution against the church which was at Jerusalem; and they were all scattered abroad throughout the regions of Judaea and Samaria, except the apostles. (Acts 8:1)

The first Christian martyr was Stephen the deacon. This persecution scattered the followers of Christ to many other locations. It was this final rejection of the gospel by the Jewish nation which took place three and a half years after the death of Jesus—in the autumn of 34 A.D. Thus was completed the seven-year period that began at Jesus' baptism and the 490-year period which was designated for the Jewish nation. Thus another prophecy of Daniel was fulfilled with such precision that only the most stubborn skeptic would deny it.

As a young man, Colin attended an Easter Sunday afternoon meeting at a movie theatre in Sydney (Australia) which on Sundays was rented by the Methodist city mission. The program that afternoon featured three men—a gospel minister, a physician, and a lawyer. Each presented his unique perspective regarding the evidence that confirms with certainty that Christ rose from the tomb. For Colin, the most compelling evidence was presented by the lawyer who detailed the many pieces of evidence which led him to conclude that the resurrection of Jesus was proved far beyond any reasonable doubt. We believe that impartial researchers of the evidence can come to no other conclusion.

What a lesson for us and our readers of this book! We pray that individually we will yield our all to the saving power of our Savior, Jesus Christ.

CHAPTER 14
Old Testament Prophecies of the Capture, Trial, Torture, Crucifixion, Resurrection, and Ascension of Christ

THE Old Testament provides many prophecies surrounding the events leading to Christ's crucifixion, resurrection, and ascension to heaven.

1. After Christ had shared the first communion service in an upper room with His disciples, He led them to the garden of Gethsemane. It was in this garden that Jesus was betrayed by one of His disciples. Before the communion service was concluded, Judas Iscariot had left to seal the financial deal to betray Jesus. Here is the Old Testament prophecy.

> Yea, mine own familiar friend, in whom I trusted, which did eat of my bread, hath lifted up his heel against me. (Psalm 41:9)

This is the fulfillment of that prophecy.

> I speak not of you all: I know whom I have chosen: but that the scripture may be fulfilled, He that eateth bread with me hath lifted up his heel against me. . . . When Jesus had thus said, he was troubled in spirit, and testified, and said, Verily, verily, I say unto you, that one of you shall betray me. . . . He then lying on Jesus' breast saith unto

him, Lord, who is it? Jesus answered, He it is, to whom I shall give a sop, when I have dipped it. And when he had dipped the sop, he gave it to Judas Iscariot, the son of Simon. And after the sop Satan entered into him. Then said Jesus unto him, That thou doest, do quickly. (John 13:18, 21, 25–27)

And while he yet spake, lo, Judas, one of the twelve, came, and with him a great multitude with swords and staves, from the chief priests and elders of the people. Now he that betrayed him gave them a sign, saying, Whomsoever I shall kiss, that same is he: hold him fast. And forthwith he came to Jesus, and said, Hail, master; and kissed him. And Jesus said unto him, Friend, wherefore art thou come? Then came they, and laid hands on Jesus, and took him. (Matthew 26:47–50)

2. It was prophesied that Christ's disciples would forsake Him.

Awake, O sword, against my shepherd, and against the man that is my fellow, saith the LORD of hosts: smite the shepherd, and the sheep shall be scattered: and I will turn mine hand upon the little ones. (Zechariah 13:7)

Here is the fulfillment of this prophecy.

Then saith Jesus unto them, All ye shall be offended because of me this night: for it is written, I will smite the shepherd, and the sheep of the flock shall be scattered abroad. . . . Peter answered and said unto him, Though all men shall be offended because of thee, yet will I never be offended. . . . Though I should die with thee, yet will I not deny thee. Likewise also said all the disciples. (Matthew 26:31–35)

> But all this was done, that the scriptures of the prophets might be fulfilled. Then all the disciples forsook him, and fled. (Matthew 26:56)

3. At His trial the religious leaders paid false witnesses to lay false accusations against Jesus. This fulfilled an Old Testament prophecy.

> False witnesses did rise up; they laid to my charge things that I knew not. (Psalm 35:11)

Here is the fulfillment of the prophecy revealed by Mark.

> And there arose certain, and bare false witness against him, saying, We heard him say, I will destroy this temple that is made with hands, and within three days I will build another made without hands. (Mark 14:57–58)

4. At His trial Jesus was scorned and mocked, fulfilling yet another Old Testament prophecy.

> All they that see me laugh me to scorn: they shoot out the lip, they shake the head, saying, He trusted on the LORD that he would deliver him: let him deliver him, seeing he delighted in him. (Psalm 22:7–8)

Here is the record of what actually took place.

> And the people stood beholding. And the rulers also with them derided him, saying, He saved others; let him save himself, if he be Christ, the chosen of God. (Luke 23:35)

5. That Christ would be beaten and tortured was also foreseen.

> Surely he hath borne our griefs, and carried our sorrows: yet we did esteem him stricken, smitten of God, and afflicted. But he was wounded for our transgressions, he was bruised for our iniquities: the chastisement of our peace was upon him; and with his stripes we are healed. (Isaiah 53:4–5)

Below is the fulfillment of what Christ suffered.

> Then did they spit in his face, and buffeted him; and others smote him with the palms of their hands, saying, Prophesy unto us, thou Christ, Who is he that smote thee? (Matthew 26:67–68)

> Then Pilate therefore took Jesus, and scourged him. And the soldiers platted a crown of thorns, and put it on his head, and they put on him a purple robe. (John 19:1–2)

6. Isaiah prophesied that the Messiah would remain silent when He was accused.

> He was oppressed, and he was afflicted, yet he opened not his mouth: he is brought as a lamb to the slaughter, and as a sheep before her shearers is dumb, so he openeth not his mouth. (Isaiah 53:7)

The Lord refused to defend Himself during His trial.

> And Pilate asked him again, saying, Answerest thou nothing? behold how many things they witness against thee. But Jesus yet answered nothing; so that Pilate marvelled. (Mark 15:4–5)

7. Jesus' death was foretold.

> He was taken from prison and from judgment: and who shall declare his generation? for he was cut off out of the land of the living: for the transgression of my people was he stricken. (Isaiah 53:8)

8. The soldiers' gambling for Christ's coat was also prophesied by David.

> They part my garments among them, and cast lots upon my vesture. (Psalm 22:18)

Here is the fulfillment of the prophecy.

> And they crucified him, and parted his garments, casting lots: that it might be fulfilled which was spoken by the prophet, They parted my garments among them, and upon my vesture did they cast lots. (Matthew 27:35)

9. Christ was given vinegar to drink, and this was yet another prophecy from the Psalms.

> They gave me also gall for my meat; and in my thirst they gave me vinegar to drink. (Psalm 69:21)

Like other such prophecies concerning Christ, this was fulfilled to the letter.

> They gave him vinegar to drink mingled with gall: and when he had tasted thereof, he would not drink. (Matthew 27:34)

10. Yet another prophecy in the Psalms said that Jesus would live what He preached.

> For my love they are my adversaries: but I give myself unto prayer. (Psalm 109:4)

Jesus had admonished His followers to love and pray for their enemies.

> But I say unto you, Love your enemies, bless them that curse you, do good to them that hate you, and pray for them which despitefully use you, and persecute you. (Matthew 5:44)

As He was dying, Jesus prayed for those who were crucifying Him.

> Then said Jesus, Father, forgive them; for they know not what they do. And they parted his raiment, and cast lots. (Luke 23:34)

11. Jesus was not crucified alone. Beside Him were two thieves.

> Therefore will I divide him a portion with the great, and he shall divide the spoil with the strong; because he hath poured out his soul unto death: and he was numbered with the transgressors; and he bare the sin of many, and made intercession for the transgressors. (Isaiah 53:12)

Here is the New Testament fulfillment.

> And when they were come to the place, which is called Calvary, there they crucified him, and the malefactors, one on the right hand, and the other on the left. (Luke 23:33)

12. The death by crucifixion was foreseen by the prophet Zechariah.

> And I will pour upon the house of David, and upon the inhabitants of Jerusalem, the spirit of grace and of supplications: and they shall look upon me whom they have pierced, and they shall mourn for him, as one mourneth for his only son, and shall be in bitterness for him, as one that is in bitterness for his firstborn. (Zechariah 12:10)

Before Jesus was taken off the cross, a soldier pierced Jesus' side instead of breaking His legs. After Christ's resurrection He offered the proof of His crucifixion and the wound left by the scar of the spear in His side.

> Then saith he to Thomas, Reach hither thy finger, and behold my hands; and reach hither thy hand, and thrust it into my side: and be not faithless, but believing. (John 20:27)

13. Jesus literally died of a broken heart.

> I am poured out like water, and all my bones are out of joint: my heart is like wax; it is melted in the midst of my bowels. (Psalm 22:14)

John the beloved disciple recorded the literal fulfillment of this prophecy.

> But one of the soldiers with a spear pierced his side, and forthwith came there out blood and water. (John 19:34)

14. In spite of His wounds, not one bone of His body was broken, though the legs of the thieves were deliberately broken.

> He keepeth all his bones: not one of them is broken. (Psalm 34:20)

John records:

> Then came the soldiers, and brake the legs of the first, and of the other which was crucified with him. But when they came to Jesus, and saw that he was dead already, they brake not his legs. . . . For these things were done, that the scripture should be fulfilled, A bone of him shall not be broken. (John 19:32–36)

15. The tomb in which Jesus' body was laid was provided by the wealthy Joseph of Arimathaea as predicted by Isaiah.

> And he made his grave with the wicked, and with the rich in his death; because he had done no violence, neither was any deceit in his mouth. (Isaiah 53:9)

Here again is the fulfillment.

> When the even was come, there came a rich man of Arimathaea, named Joseph, who also himself was Jesus' disciple: he went to Pilate, and begged the body of Jesus. Then Pilate commanded the body to be delivered. And when Joseph had taken the body, he wrapped it in a clean linen cloth, and laid it in his own new tomb, which he had hewn out in the rock: and he rolled a great stone to the door of the sepulchre, and departed. (Matthew 27:57–60)

16. It was foretold that He would be resurrected from the dead.

> For thou wilt not leave my soul in hell; neither wilt thou suffer thine Holy One to see corruption. (Psalm 16:10)

> But God will redeem my soul from the power of the grave: for he shall receive me. (Psalm 49:15)

The record of His resurrection is very explicit. When Peter was speaking to the Jews at Pentecost, He quoted a prophecy of David concerning Christ:

> Therefore did my heart rejoice, and my tongue was glad; moreover also my flesh shall rest in hope: because thou wilt not leave my soul in hell, neither wilt thou suffer thine Holy One to see corruption. Thou hast made known to me the ways of life; thou shalt make me full of joy with thy countenance. Men and brethren, let me freely speak unto you of the patriarch David, that he is both dead and buried, and his sepulchre is with us unto this day. Therefore being a prophet, and knowing that God had sworn with an oath to him, that of the fruit of his loins, according to the flesh, he would raise up Christ to sit on his throne; he seeing this before spake of the resurrection of Christ, that his soul was not left in hell, neither his flesh did see corruption. (Acts 2:26–31)

17. His ascension to heaven was also prophesied.

> Thou hast ascended on high, thou hast led captivity captive: thou hast received gifts for men; yea, for the rebellious also, that the Lord God might dwell among them. (Psalm 68:18)

Here is the record of that ascension.

> So then after the Lord had spoken unto them, he was received up into heaven, and sat on the right hand of God. (Mark 16:19)

18. In heaven Christ is our heavenly high priest.

> The LORD hath sworn, and will not repent, Thou art a priest for ever after the order of Melchizedek. (Psalm 110:4)

The New Testament confirms His high-priestly ministry.

> So also Christ glorified not himself to be made an high priest; but he that said unto him, Thou art my Son, to day have I begotten thee. As he saith also in another place, Thou art a priest for ever after the order of Melchisedec. (Hebrews 5:5–6)

It is important to note that Jesus is not a Levitical priest but after the higher order of Melchisedec, for He was not born into the tribe of Levi. Remember, He was born of the tribe of Judah.

How faithfully Jesus' birth, life, death, resurrection, and ascension to heaven fulfilled the Old Testament prophecies!

CHAPTER 15
What About Unfulfilled Prophecies?

SOME skeptics point to the fact that a number of the Bible prophecies have not been fulfilled. First we must differentiate between those prophecies which were unfulfilled and those which *as yet, have not been fulfilled*. In this latter category are those prophecies relating to future events such as the return of Christ, the events during the millennium, the destruction of the wicked, and the recreation of this world.

We will first address what is probably the best-known unfulfilled prophecy—Jonah's prediction of the destruction of Assyria's capital, Nineveh. For Christian children who have been faithfully instructed, this story is well known before they reach teenage years. Assyria was near the zenith of its power, and at this time, it was the most powerful nation in the world, dominating the Middle East and North Africa. The Bible record declares that Jonah was called of God to warn the Ninevites of their impending destruction.

> Now the word of the LORD came unto Jonah the son of Amittai, saying, Arise, go to Nineveh, that great city, and cry against it; for their wickedness is come up before me. (Jonah 1:1–2)

Jonah, no doubt because of his great fear of giving such a frightening message, fled in the opposite direction, boarding a boat at Joppa which was traveling to Tarshish. The story tells of a fearful storm and the sailors' search for a scapegoat. Jonah was awakened, and lots were cast to determine the one responsible for the curse which caused the terrible storm. The lot fell upon Jonah, who confessed that he was responsible for God's displeasure upon him. He agreed to be cast overboard. His ordeal of three days and nights in a large fish's belly, his being vomited up on dry land, and his subsequent willingness to give God's fearful warning to the Ninevites is told in the first two chapters of the Bible book of Jonah.

> But the LORD sent out a great wind into the sea, and there was a mighty tempest in the sea, so that the ship was like to be broken. Then the mariners were afraid, and cried every man unto his god, and cast forth the wares that were in the ship into the sea, to lighten it of them. But Jonah was gone down into the sides of the ship; and he lay, and was fast asleep. So the shipmaster came to him, and said unto him, What meanest thou, O sleeper? arise, call upon thy God, if so be that God will think upon us, that we perish not. And they said every one to his fellow, Come, and let us cast lots, that we may know for whose cause this evil is upon us. So they cast lots, and the lot fell upon Jonah.
>
> Then said they unto him, Tell us, we pray thee, for whose cause this evil is upon us; What is thine occupation? and whence comest thou? what is thy country? and of what people art thou? And he said unto them, I am an Hebrew; and I fear the LORD, the God of heaven, which hath made the sea and the dry land. Then were the men exceedingly afraid, and said unto him, Why hast thou done this? For the men knew that he fled from the presence of the LORD, because he had told them. Then said they unto him, What shall we do unto thee, that the sea may be calm unto us? for the sea wrought, and was tempestuous. And he said unto them, Take me up, and cast me forth into the sea; so shall the sea be calm unto you: for I know that for my sake this great tempest is upon you. Nevertheless the men rowed hard to bring it to the land; but they could not: for the sea wrought, and was tempestuous against

them. Wherefore they cried unto the Lord, and said, We beseech thee, O Lord, we beseech thee, let us not perish for this man's life, and lay not upon us innocent blood: for thou, O Lord, hast done as it pleased thee. So they took up Jonah, and cast him forth into the sea: and the sea ceased from her raging.

Then the men feared the Lord exceedingly, and offered a sacrifice unto the Lord, and made vows. Now the Lord had prepared a great fish to swallow up Jonah. And Jonah was in the belly of the fish three days and three nights.

Then Jonah prayed unto the Lord his God out of the fish's belly, and said, I cried by reason of mine affliction unto the Lord, and he heard me; out of the belly of hell cried I, and thou heardest my voice. For thou hadst cast me into the deep, in the midst of the seas; and the floods compassed me about: all thy billows and thy waves passed over me. Then I said, I am cast out of thy sight; yet I will look again toward thy holy temple. The waters compassed me about, even to the soul: the depth closed me round about, the weeds were wrapped about my head. I went down to the bottoms of the mountains; the earth with her bars was about me for ever: yet hast thou brought up my life from corruption, O Lord my God. When my soul fainted within me I remembered the Lord: and my prayer came in unto thee, into thine holy temple. They that observe lying vanities forsake their own mercy. But I will sacrifice unto thee with the voice of thanksgiving; I will pay that that I have vowed. Salvation is of the Lord. And the Lord spake unto the fish, and it vomited out Jonah upon the dry land. (Jonah 1:4–2:10)

It took Jonah three days to reach Nineveh, which was located on the north side of the Tigris River, close to where the city of Mosul is now located on the south side of the Tigris river. Now, however, Jonah was given another important detail—that 40 days after he gave the warning message, Nineveh would be destroyed. The issue here is the 40 days. If God had simply told Jonah that the city of Nineveh would be destroyed, there would be no problem, for the city was destroyed much later by the Medes in the year 612 B.C. (See "Nineveh." *Encyclopædia Britannica 2007 Ultimate Reference Suite.*) However, Jonah faithfully gave the warning to the people, and then he waited, no doubt at a distance, for the destruction to come. The destruction did not take place, and Jonah was greatly displeased with God, no doubt because he believed that his credibility has been gravely damaged. Here is the record.

> But it displeased Jonah exceedingly, and he was very angry. And he prayed unto the LORD, and said, I pray thee, O LORD, was not this my saying, when I was yet in my country? Therefore I fled before unto Tarshish: for I knew that thou art a gracious God, and merciful, slow to anger, and of great kindness, and repentest thee of the evil. Therefore now, O LORD, take, I beseech thee, my life from me; for it is better for me to die than to live. (Jonah 4:1–3)

Well might we conclude that here is a time prophecy which was not fulfilled. It might be deduced that such prophecies do not depict an all-knowing God, or at the least that some prophecies are not reliable. However, that conclusion would be too hasty.

Remember that God is a merciful and longsuffering God.

> O give thanks unto the LORD; for he is good; for his mercy endureth for ever. (1 Chronicles 16:34)

> But God, who is rich in mercy, for his great love wherewith he loved us. (Ephesians 2:4)

> And the LORD passed by before him, and proclaimed, The LORD, The LORD God, merciful and gracious, longsuffering, and abundant in goodness and truth. (Exodus 34:6)

> And account that the longsuffering of our Lord is salvation; even as our beloved brother Paul also according to the wisdom given unto him hath written unto you. (2 Peter 3:15)

As a merciful and longsuffering God to the human race, He warns of impending tragic consequences primarily to provide an opportunity for individuals, groups, cities, nations, and ultimately the world, to redress their wickedness, evil cruelties, and rebellion against God. If there is a turning away from their iniquity, God stays the terrible consequences which would otherwise befall them.

In other words, many of the Bible prophecies are conditional. Prophecies of punishment are unfulfilled and dire consequences are staid when man turns back to God, and promises of protection and prosperity are unfulfilled when people reject the counsel of the Lord and thereby forfeit God's blessings.

Let us review some such prophecies. The very first of these prophecies was given to our first parents.

> And the LORD God took the man, and put him into the garden of Eden to dress it and to keep it. And the LORD God commanded the man, saying, Of every tree of the garden thou mayest freely eat: but of the tree of the knowledge of good and evil, thou shalt not eat of it: for in the day that thou eatest thereof thou shalt surely die. (Genesis 2:15–17)

God not only warned the Edenic couple not to eat of the fruit of the tree of the knowledge of good and evil, He specified the fearful consequences if they did eat of that fruit. With terrible bitterness, they suffered the dire consequences of disregarding this loving warning of God.

Also, the prophet Jeremiah was given a conditional prophecy which he gave to the Jewish leaders and people.

> Thus saith the LORD; Stand in the court of the LORD's house, and speak unto all the cities of Judah, which come

> to worship in the LORD's house, all the words that I command thee to speak unto them; diminish not a word: if so be they will hearken, and turn every man from his evil way, that I may repent me of the evil, which I purpose to do unto them because of the evil of their doings. And thou shalt say unto them, Thus saith the LORD; If ye will not hearken to me, to walk in my law, which I have set before you, to hearken to the words of my servants the prophets, whom I sent unto you, both rising up early, and sending them, but ye have not hearkened; then will I make this house like Shiloh, and will make this city a curse to all the nations of the earth. (Jeremiah 26:2–6)

After the priests, the prophets, and all the people decided that Jeremiah should be executed for the deliverance of this message, the princes providentially and wisely refused to carry out this threat against Jeremiah.

> Now it came to pass, when Jeremiah had made an end of speaking all that the LORD had commanded him to speak unto all the people, that the priests and the prophets and all the people took him, saying, Thou shalt surely die.... Then said the princes and all the people unto the priests and to the prophets; This man is not worthy to die: for he hath spoken to us in the name of the LORD our God. (Jeremiah 26:8, 16)

Thus God preserved Jerusalem at that time. However, later civil leaders returned to their open rebellion against God, and at that time they were brutally attacked by Nebuchadnezzar in 605 B.C. Even then, God did not permit Nebuchadnezzar to destroy Jerusalem completely. Because of the death of his father, Nabopolassar, Nebuchadnezzar had to return to Babylon to secure the throne. Indeed, even at the time of Nebuchadnezzar's second invasion in 597 B.C., the temple was not damaged. However, ultimately the failure of the Jews to return to the God of their salvation resulted in the total destruction of Jerusalem, and the magnificent temple built by Solomon was wholly left in ruins in 586 B.C.

Thus, eventually God's prophecy through Jeremiah was sadly fulfilled because of the impenitence of the Jews.

Now referring back to the prophecy of Jonah. God gave a similar grace period for this pagan city of Nineveh to embrace the worship of the true God. Why did not God destroy Nineveh after the 40 days? The answer is plainly recorded in Scripture.

> So the people of Nineveh believed God, and proclaimed a fast, and put on sackcloth, from the greatest of them even to the least of them. For word came unto the king of Nineveh, and he arose from his throne, and he laid his robe from him, and covered him with sackcloth, and sat in ashes. And he caused it to be proclaimed and published through Nineveh by the decree of the king and his nobles, saying, Let neither man nor beast, herd nor flock, taste any thing: let them not feed, nor drink water: but let man and beast be covered with sackcloth, and cry mightily unto God: yea, let them turn every one from his evil way, and from the violence that is in their hands. Who can tell if God will turn and repent, and turn away from his fierce anger, that we perish not? And God saw their works, that they turned from their evil way; and God repented of the evil, that he had said that he would do unto them; and he did it not. (Jonah 3:5–10)

Some Bible exponents believe this event took place during the reign of King Adad-nirari III (810–782 B.C.). Some Bible students assume that God's mercy was exercised only to His chosen people, the Israelites and Jews. However, this is far from the truth. God also sought to woo pagan peoples by His love.

It will be noted that God had mercy upon the Ninevites even though the inhabitants were from a heathen city. Sadly, Jonah the prophet was not pleased with God's longsuffering.

> But it displeased Jonah exceedingly, and he was very angry. (Jonah 4:1)

Tragically, the Ninevites returned to their idolatry, and eventually the city was destroyed by the Medes in 612 B.C. God's love in His efforts to save Nineveh and the entire nation of Assyria is seen in the fact that He commissioned another prophet, Nahum, to warn the whole nation of its impending defeat and destruction.

> And it shall come to pass, that all they that look upon thee shall flee from thee, and say, Nineveh is laid waste: who will bemoan her? whence shall I seek comforters for thee? . . . Thy crowned are as the locusts, and thy captains as the great grasshoppers, which camp in the hedges in the cold day, but when the sun ariseth they flee away, and their place is not known where they are. Thy shepherds slumber, O king of Assyria: thy nobles shall dwell in the dust: thy people is scattered upon the mountains, and no man gathereth them. There is no healing of thy bruise; thy wound is grievous: all that hear the bruit of thee shall clap the hands over thee: for upon whom hath not thy wickedness passed continually? (Nahum 3:7, 17–19)

However, the Assyrians did not repent as they had when Jonah prophesied. Thus, God sadly withdrew His protection, and the prophecy of Nahum was fulfilled.

CHAPTER 16
Yet-to-Be-Fulfilled Prophecies

WE believe that we have presented incontrovertible evidence that God's prophecies are not fictitious, man-devised predictions or human speculations. When we observe the indisputable confirmation of biblical prophecy by the events of realized history, only the most determined atheists could deny the evidence.

Both the authors did extensive studies on statistical probability in our university courses. While we cannot hazard a guess as to the probability of all the presented prophetic fulfillments which we have provided in this book being fulfilled by chance, we know that it would be so infinitesimal as to be wholly implausible. The probability would be perhaps as remote as the probability of evolution accounting for the existence of the universe.

God has provided prophecy not only to acquaint us with the consequences of following His life or defying His loving invitation to serve Him, but also to prove beyond any doubt that there is an all-knowing Creator-God of the universe.

> Daniel answered and said, Blessed be the name of God for ever and ever: for wisdom and might are his: and he changeth the times and the seasons: he removeth kings, and setteth up kings: he giveth wisdom unto the wise, and knowledge to them that know understanding: he revealeth the deep and secret things: he knoweth what is in the darkness, and the light dwelleth with him. (Daniel 2:20–22)

> But there is a God in heaven that revealeth secrets, and maketh known to the king Nebuchadnezzar what shall be in the latter days.... (Daniel 2:28)
>
> Surely the Lord GOD will do nothing, but he revealeth his secret unto his servants the prophets. (Amos 3:7)
>
> Let all the nations be gathered together, and let the people be assembled: who among them can declare this, and shew us former things? let them bring forth their witnesses, that they may be justified: or let them hear, and say, It is truth. (Isaiah 43:9)
>
> The Revelation of Jesus Christ, which God gave unto him, to shew unto his servants things which must shortly come to pass.... (Revelation 1:1)

We have presented some of the prophecies which have been fulfilled in every minute detail. We present this evidence so that the readers of this book who have faith in God will have their faith strengthened and so that other honest men and women who have had preconceived disbelief in God based upon ignorance of the Scriptures or upon false premises will seek to find their way to the God of their salvation. This book has also been written to help those who have been uncertain or undecided concerning the veracity of God's Word.

What a difference there is between the certainties of the Bible and the uncertainties of non-God-inspired prophets! Many, for example, become ecstatic over the prognostications of Nostradamus (1503–1566), Edgar Cayce, and Jeane Dixon. How vague and unclear are many of Nostradamus' predictions! Where is the clarity and pinpoint accuracy as is evidenced in the 70-week prophecy of Daniel 9 or the 1,260-year prophecy? Also, let us compare the fulfillment of modern-day "prophets." Every new year, tabloids present the predictions for the upcoming year, most of which never eventuate. At best, at the completion of the year we may find the percentage of these "prophecies" which were fulfilled. In our estimation, often some "fulfillments" are very doubtful. However, we agree that a small percentage of these predictions are fulfilled. Yet, in reality, any astute and well-informed individual could predict the likelihood of some events which could take place the following year. For example, we were completing this manuscript at the end of 2007 and the beginning of 2008. Surely many would be able to predict the choice of the next President of the United States. A much smaller group may even predict accurately who will be elected the Vice-President. However, it would be unlikely that anyone could predict who will comprise the cabinet ministers—maybe not even the presidential candidates themselves. What is the likelihood that anyone could accurately predict all the representatives and senators who will be elected or reelected?

What are the fulfilled prophecies of other religions? Where are the fulfilled prophecies in the writings, for example, of the Muslim Koran, the philosophies of Buddha, the writings of the Hindus or those of Confucius? The Word of God is very precise and stands alone, which is evidence of its divine credentials. Remember, many of the prophecies which we have presented have stood the test of millennia, predicting events that were centuries in the future, not just the coming year. How could Daniel have prophesied what is clear to us today, that the medieval reign of the papacy would end in 1798, well over 2,000 years before it happened? How could John the Revelator prophesy the same event about seventeen hundred years before it transpired and then foretell the amazing, powerful restoration of this power which many thought was destroyed forever at the time of its "deadly wound"? There is certainly "a God in heaven that revealeth secrets" (Daniel 2:28) unto His servants the prophets.

In this book we have explored only a sample of the most outstanding biblical prophecies. We could have explored other prophecies perhaps not so dramatic. For example, there was the prophecy that the freed Israelite slaves of Egypt would languish in the desert for forty years before they inhabited the promised land of Canaan:

> But your little ones, which ye said should be a prey, them will I bring in, and they shall know the land which ye have despised. But as for you, your carcases, they shall fall in this

wilderness. And your children shall wander in the wilderness forty years, and bear your whoredoms, until your carcases be wasted in the wilderness. (Numbers 14:31–33)

Another prophecy said the Jews would be in captivity in Babylon for seventy years.

And this whole land shall be a desolation, and an astonishment; and these nations shall serve the king of Babylon seventy years. (Jeremiah 25:11)

A further remarkable prophecy was God's assurance to Gideon that 300 men of Israel would defeat the mighty army of the Midianites.

And the LORD said unto Gideon, By the three hundred men that lapped will I save you, and deliver the Midianites into thine hand: and let all the other people go every man unto his place. . . . And the three hundred blew the trumpets, and the LORD set every man's sword against his fellow, even throughout all the host [of the Midianites]: and the host fled to Bethshittah in Zererath, and to the border of Abelmeholah, unto Tabbath. (Judges 7:7, 22)

There is a myriad of other diverse prophecies which were fulfilled in Bible times.

Thus we now address yet-to-be-fulfilled prophecies. Because of the fulfillment of prophecies in past history, those of us who are living toward the end of this wicked world's journey have no excuse to deny confidence that those prophecies that are focused on the end of this sin-blighted earth's history will be fulfilled with the same pin-point accuracy as the divine prophecies of the past. We earnestly hope that our readers will not only give intellectual consent to the validity of these yet-to-be-fulfilled prophecies, but that each reader will surrender his will to the mighty love of the all-powerful, all-knowing God of the universe who sent His beloved Son to die to rescue the human race from its otherwise inevitable destruction. The gratitude we owe God should evoke our total allegiance to Him.

We will address just a few chosen yet-to-be-fulfilled prophecies which will with certainty be fulfilled in the not-too-distant future. We will begin with Christ's prophecy of long ago concerning events which will transpire immediately preceding His second coming to redeem the saints of all ages.

The disciples, at that time, did not differentiate between the destruction of Jerusalem and its temple on the one hand and the return of Jesus at His second coming on the other hand. Here are their questions.

> And as he sat upon the mount of Olives, the disciples came unto him privately, saying, Tell us, when shall these things be? and what shall be the sign of thy coming, and of the end of the world? (Matthew 24:3)

Jesus gave His prophetic response by combining these two events, no doubt, because they were similar, especially in the destructive phase of the two events. Thus in some ways the destruction of Jerusalem was a type of the vastly greater devastation of the world just before the return of Jesus. As we have detailed in the chapter entitled "The Years of Christ's Ministry and Sacrifice Foretold," the city and the temple were destroyed in A.D. 70 by the Roman army under the leadership of Titus. Just as surely, this world will be destroyed comprehensively when the seven last plagues are poured out. See Revelation 16. We will quote here only the destruction under the seventh plague.

> And the seventh angel poured out his vial into the air; and there came a great voice out of the temple of heaven, from the throne, saying, It is done. And there were voices, and thunders, and lightnings; and there was a great earthquake, such as was not since men were upon the earth, so mighty an earthquake, and so great. And the great city was divided into three parts, and the cities of the nations fell: and great Babylon came in remembrance

before God, to give unto her the cup of the wine of the fierceness of his wrath. And every island fled away, and the mountains were not found. And there fell upon men a great hail out of heaven, every stone about the weight of a talent: and men blasphemed God because of the plague of the hail; for the plague thereof was exceeding great. (Revelation 16:17–21)

Some may not understand that the reference to Babylon is not a reference to the ancient city of Babylon, for it was destroyed eternally, as is explained in the chapter entitled "Babylon, the City Which Cannot Be Rebuilt." We must understand that Babylon was the pseudonym for Rome which was used by John the Revelator because it would have been exceedingly dangerous to write these prophecies using the name of the city of Rome at the time when the Roman Empire was at its zenith. It will be impossible for earthly leaders to solve the terrible carnage, deaths, and chaos in society as we approach the end of this world's history. No wonder Jesus said,

And there shall be signs in the sun, and in the moon, and in the stars; and upon the earth distress of nations, with perplexity; the sea and the waves roaring; men's hearts failing them for fear, and for looking after those things which are coming on the earth: for the powers of heaven shall be shaken. (Luke 21:25–26)

The only safety at this time will be for those who are under the loving protection of our Savior, Jesus Christ. Tragic though these events will be, to God's people they will be seen as the sure sign that Jesus is soon to return, and in this will be their assurance.

And then shall they see the Son of man coming in a cloud with power and great glory. And when these things begin to come to pass, then look up, and lift up your heads; for your redemption draweth nigh. (Luke 21:27–28)

Prior to the return of Jesus there will be fearful attempts to destroy God's people. Led by the papacy and supported by other religious bodies, every effort will be exercised to coerce the whole human race to receive the mark of the papacy's authority—Sunday sacredness.

> And he had power to give life unto the image of the beast, that the image of the beast should both speak, and cause that as many as would not worship the image of the beast should be killed. And he causeth all, both small and great, rich and poor, free and bond, to receive a mark in their right hand, or in their foreheads: and that no man might buy or sell, save he that had the mark, or the name of the beast, or the number of his name. (Revelation 13:15–17)

Tragically there will be many faithful martyrs just prior to the time when Christ will cease to intercede for sinners. Those who have surrendered their will to the Lord, on the one hand, will be so completely loyal to Christ that nothing will induce or threaten them away from His side. On the other hand, the vast majority of humanity will be so resistant to God's final appeal to the human race that no further loving entreaties would alter their rejection of salvation's grace. Then comes the divine declaration which seals the destiny of each human being for eternity.

> He that is unjust, let him be unjust still: and he which is filthy, let him be filthy still: and he that is righteous, let him be righteous still: and he that is holy, let him be holy still. (Revelation 22:11)

The destiny of all who follow the false religion of the papacy will be decided for eternal destruction.

> . . . The Lord Jesus shall be revealed from heaven with his mighty angels, in flaming fire taking vengeance on them that know not God, and that obey not the gospel

of our Lord Jesus Christ: who shall be punished with everlasting destruction from the presence of the Lord, and from the glory of his power. (2 Thessalonians 1: 7–9)

Before the return of Christ, the papacy will be ruthlessly destroyed by those who have been deceived by the false claims of the papacy.

And the great city was divided into three parts, and the cities of the nations fell: and great Babylon came in remembrance before God, to give unto her the cup of the wine of the fierceness of his wrath. (Revelation 16:19)

And the ten horns which thou sawest upon the beast, these shall hate the whore, and shall make her desolate and naked, and shall eat her flesh, and burn her with fire. For God hath put in their hearts to fulfil his will, and to agree, and give their kingdom unto the beast, until the words of God shall be fulfilled. (Revelation 17:16–17)

In this book we have not only attempted to prove beyond any reasonable doubt that there is an all-knowing God, the Creator of the universe, who has revealed remarkable future events in the Bible which defy rational explanations apart from Him; we have also sought to lead you to God through His Son who died for your salvation so that you may be among His faithful ones who will live with Him eternally. We pray that this will be your experience. We hope to meet you there.

Index

Bible References

Genesis 2:15-17	127
Genesis 9:11	108
Genesis 10:8-12	14
Genesis 10:9-10	15
Genesis 10:11-12	16
Genesis 13:10-12	9
Genesis 13:13	10
Genesis 14:1-2	10
Genesis 14:21-23	10
Genesis 18:23-25	11
Genesis 18:26	11
Genesis 18:28-32	12
Genesis 19:4-5	12
Genesis 19:26	12
Genesis 49:10	91
Exodus 34:6	126
Numbers 14:31-33	134
Numbers 14:34	48, 68, 103
Judges 7:7, 22	134
1 Kings 14:24	13
1 Chronicles 16:34	126
Ezra 6:14	105
Ezra 7:7	105
Psalm 16:10	121
Psalm 22:7-8	115
Psalm 22:14	119
Psalm 22:18	117
Psalm 34:20	120
Psalm 35:11	115
Psalm 41:9	113
Psalm 49:15	121
Psalm 68:18	121
Psalm 69:21	117
Psalm 109:4	118
Psalm 110:4	122
Isaiah 1:4	83
Isaiah 1:7	83
Isaiah 1:9	83
Isaiah 7:14	94
Isaiah 9:1-2	92
Isaiah 11:10	91
Isaiah 11:11	15
Isaiah 13:19-20	13
Isaiah 13:19-21	75, 79
Isaiah 21:9	75
Isaiah 37:36-37	16
Isaiah 37:37-38	17
Isaiah 40:3-5	97
Isaiah 43:8-12	8
Isaiah 43:9	132
Isaiah 53:4-5	116
Isaiah 53:7	116
Isaiah 53:8	117
Isaiah 53:9	120
Isaiah 53:12	118
Isaiah 56:7	98
Jeremiah 4:27	87
Jeremiah 7:11	98
Jeremiah 9:2-3	84
Jeremiah 25:11	83, 134
Jeremiah 25:25	79
Jeremiah 25:29	87
Jeremiah 26:2-6	128
Jeremiah 26:8, 16	128
Jeremiah 27:22	85
Jeremiah 29:14	86
Jeremiah 30:2-3	85

Jeremiah 30:3 86	Daniel 7:25 47
Jeremiah 30:11 87	Daniel 8:1-5 36
Jeremiah 30:18 86	Daniel 8:3, 5, 8 103
Jeremiah 31:15 95	Daniel 8:4 39
Jeremiah 33:3 86	Daniel 8:5-7 40
Jeremiah 46:27-28 88	Daniel 8:8 . . . . 40, 41
Jeremiah 49:18 13	Daniel 8:9 42
Jeremiah 50:3 79	Daniel 8:16 37
Jeremiah 50:17 84	Daniel 8:20-21 38
Jeremiah 50:18 85	Daniel 8:21 40
Jeremiah 50:19 . . . . 85, 87	Daniel 8:22 41
Jeremiah 50:38 78	Daniel 8:23-24 42
Jeremiah 50:39 77	Daniel 8:25 43
Jeremiah 50:40 . . . . 13, 76	Daniel 9:21-27 104
Jeremiah 51:5 88	Daniel 9:24 . . . . 106, 109
Jeremiah 51:8 . . . . 76, 78	Daniel 9:25 105
Jeremiah 51:11 79	Daniel 9:26 . . . . 108, 110
Jeremiah 51:24 87	Daniel 9:27 108
Jeremiah 51:24-25 78	Daniel 12:7 47
Jeremiah 51:28 79	Hosea 11:1 95
Jeremiah 51:29 77	Amos 3:7 132
Jeremiah 51:37 77	Amos 9:14-15 86
Jeremiah 51:43 78	Jonah 1:1-2 123
Jeremiah 51:62 . . . . 77, 80	Jonah 1:4-2:10 125
Ezekiel 4:6 . . . . 49, 68, 103	Jonah 3:5-10 129
Daniel 1:1-2 15	Jonah 3:10 18
Daniel 1:12, 14 23	Jonah 4:1 129
Daniel 1:19-20 23	Jonah 4:1-3 126
Daniel 2:2 24	Micah 5:2 93
Daniel 2:12-13 24	Nahum 3:7 18
Daniel 2:15 24	Nahum 3:7, 17-19 130
Daniel 2:16-23 25	Zechariah 9:9 98
Daniel 2:20-22 131	Zechariah 12:10 119
Daniel 2:22 101	Zechariah 13:7 114
Daniel 2:24 25	Matthew 1:1-3, 16 92
Daniel 2:25 25	Matthew 1:23 94
Daniel 2:27-28 26	Matthew 2:12-13 95
Daniel 2:28 132	Matthew 2:14-15 96
Daniel 2:31-35 26	Matthew 2:16-18 95
Daniel 2:38-44 27	Matthew 3:1-3 97
Daniel 2:42 102	Matthew 3:9 39
Daniel 2:43 29	Matthew 3:13-17 107
Daniel 3:2 82	Matthew 4:13-16 92
Daniel 5:30-31 74	Matthew 5:44 118
Daniel 7:7 30	Matthew 9:2-3 66
Daniel 7:8 . . . . 34, 42	Matthew 17:1-5 6
Daniel 7:24 102	Matthew 21:12-13 98

Index

Matthew 21:17-19	110
Matthew 23:37-38	111
Matthew 24:1-2	111
Matthew 24:3	135
Matthew 26:31-35	114
Matthew 26:47-50	114
Matthew 26:56	115
Matthew 26:63-65	66
Matthew 26:67-68	116
Matthew 27:34	117
Matthew 27:35	117
Matthew 27:57-60	120
Mark 1:15	107
Mark 11:7-11	99
Mark 14:57-58	115
Mark 15:4-5	116
Mark 16:19	122
Luke 1:30, 34-35	94
Luke 2:1-7, 11	93
Luke 2:25-34	96
Luke 2:36-38	97
Luke 3:23-33	92
Luke 19:41-44	110
Luke 21:25-26	136
Luke 21:27-28	136
Luke 23:33	118
Luke 23:34	118
Luke 23:35	115
John 13:18, 21, 25-27	114
John 19:1-2	116
John 19:14-16	109
John 19:31	109
John 19:32-36	120
John 19:34	119
John 19:38-42	100
John 20:27	119
Acts 1:8	111
Acts 2:26-31	121
Acts 4:4	111
Acts 6:7	100, 112
Acts 8:1	112
Acts 10:37-38	107
Ephesians 2:4	126
2 Thessalonians 1:7-9	138
Hebrews 5:5-6	122
1 Peter 1:24-25	81
1 Peter 5:13	75
2 Peter 1:16-21	7
2 Peter 1:19-21	101
2 Peter 3:15	127
1 John 1:1-4	6
Revelation 1:1	132
Revelation 1:8	5
Revelation 11:2	47
Revelation 11:3	47
Revelation 12:6	47
Revelation 12:14	47
Revelation 13:3	46, 53, 54, 67
Revelation 13:3-4	59
Revelation 13:5	48
Revelation 13:8	46, 55, 69
Revelation 13:11	70
Revelation 13:12, 15-16	71
Revelation 13:15-17	137
Revelation 14:8	76
Revelation 16:17-21	136
Revelation 16:19	138
Revelation 17:12-14, 16-17	60
Revelation 17:15	66
Revelation 17:16	43
Revelation 17:16-17	138
Revelation 18:2	76
Revelation 21:6	5
Revelation 22:11	137
Revelation 22:13	5

People

Abram	10
Alexander the Great	28, 31, 40
Andrews, John Nevins	70
Antigonus I	31
Antiochus III	32
Artaxerxes	105
Astyages	39
Azariah	21, 82
Belshazzar	28, 30, 35, 73
Benedict XVI	52
Berthier, General	50
Cassander	32, 41
Cayce, Edgar	132
Charlemagne	29
Cyaxares	17, 74

Cyrus 39, 74
Daniel .... .20, 24, 30, 35, 39,
.... 82, 101, 106, 112, 133
Darius 74, 79
Dixon, Jeane 132
Dougherty, Raymond 37
Einstein, Albert 45
Ezra 105
Gagarin, Yuri 64
Gaspari, Cardinal 53, 67
Graham, Billy 69
Hananiah 21, 82
Hawking, Stephen 45
Hitler, Adolph 29, 54
Hussein, Saddam 81
Isaiah 73, 79, 83, 93, 120
Jeremiah 73, 75, 79, 80, 84, 86, 128
Jewson, Edwin 57
John II, Pope 49, 68
John Paul II, Pope 43, 54
John XXIII, Pope 54
Jonah 17, 129
Justinian, Emperor 33, 49, 68
Lot (Abram's nephew) 9
Lysimachus 32, 41
Menzies, Robert Gordon 56
Merodach, Evil 38
Mishael 21, 82
Mussolini, Benito 53, 57, 67
Nabonidus 37, 38, 73
Nabopolassar 17, 20, 74, 128
Nahum 18, 130
Napoleon 29, 50
Nebuchadnezzar .... .17, 21, 30, 35,
.... 38, 73, 82, 128
Neriglissar 38
Newton, Isaac 45
Nimrod 14, 73
Nostradamus 132
Pius IX, Pope 52
Pius VI, Pope 50, 52, 67, 69
Pius VII, Pope 52
Pius XI, Pope 53
Pius XII, Pope 54
Ptolemy 31, 41
Seleucus 32, 41
Sennacherib 16, 75

Shepard, Alan 64
Standish, Darcy Roland 62
Trajan, Emperor 80
Tse-tung, Mao 63
Victoria, Queen 29
Vigilius, Pope 49, 69
Wilhelm, Kaiser 29
XII, Pope Pius 53

Other Topics

Agnostics 5, 27
Assyria 14, 75, 85, 130
Atheists 5, 27, 71, 80, 94, 131
Australia 56, 61, 63
Babylon .... .15, 17, 27, 30, 31, 37, 38,
.... 67, 73, 76, 79, 84, 89, 136
Berlin Wall 64
China 63
Cold War 65
Communism 61
Council of Orleans 49
European Union 28
Evolutionists 5
Germany 29, 56, 61
Great Britain 29, 56, 61
Islam 60, 72
Japan 57, 62
Jerusalem 73, 82, 105, 110, 128, 135
Jonah 123
Lateran Treaty 53, 67
Medo-Persia 28, 31, 38, 39, 67, 73, 79
Nineveh 14, 20, 74, 79, 85, 123, 129
Ostrogoths 28, 32, 49, 69
Pearl Harbor 56, 61
Pontifex Maximus 68
Rome 28, 32, 41, 49, 58, 67, 76, 136
Second Vatican Council 54
Shinar 15
Shushan 39
Skeptics 5, 20, 27, 36, 71, 123
Soviet Union 57, 61
United Nations 71
United States of America 60, 64, 70
World War I 29
World War II 54, 56, 61, 62, 68

Hartland Publications Book List

Note: This list is current as of the date of publication.
For an up-to-date list, please visit our web site at
http://www.hartlandpublications.com.

These books may be ordered from Hartland Publications
(see the last page of this book for complete contact information).
Many of these books are also available from Highwood Books in Australia: 03–59637011

Books by Colin Standish and Russell Standish
(Unless otherwise noted as by one or the other)

The Antichrist Is Here (187 pages)
Colin and Russell Standish have extensively researched the historical identification of the antichrist of past generations and are convinced that the antichrist is present on earth now. They have taken the events which have transpired in recent years and measured them in the light of biblical prophecy. You will read undeniable evidence in support of their findings. This book is a "must-read" for those who are interested in biblical prophecy and its outworking in contemporary history.

The Big Bang Exploded (218 pages)
For decades the "big bang" hypothesis has held sway as the dominant explanation of the origin of the universe. It has proven to be a remarkably enduring hypothesis, yet the determined efforts of scientists from many disciplines have failed to provide confirmation of this hypothesis.

The authors assert that the "big bang theory" and Darwin's proposal of natural selection are spent, decayed and archaic theories. The Standish brothers seriously address some of the most startling challenges to this theory of origins. They present evidence which they assert supports, far more closely, the fiat creation concept than the evolutionary model. This is another of the increasing challenges which evolutionary scientists must address if their credibility is not to be seriously undermined.

Education for Excellence (174 pages)

This book goes directly to the Word of God for educational principles for the sons and daughters of the King of the Universe. In the ministry of the apostle Paul, the culture, philosophy and education of paganism was confronted by the principles of God-given education. Though the world of his day was under the political rulership of Rome, Greece still controlled the mind and, therefore, the educational processes of the Mediterranean. As Paul's ministry led him to city after city under the influence of Greek education and philosophy, it was necessary for him to define clearly the differences between pagan and Christian education.

Most cultures today face the continued influence of paganistic education. Many who claim to support Christian education nevertheless are not fully aware of the complete contrasts between the two. Christianity wholly defines the curriculum, the teacher selection, the teaching methodology, the extracurricular activities, and so on. Its goals, purposes and objectives are entirely different from secular education.

The Entertainment Syndrome (118 pages)

This book explores how the large increase in entertainment impacts the physical, emotional, social, intellectual, and spiritual life of the human race and the devastating effect of its use in our churches.

The European Union, the North American Union, the Papacy, and Globalism (192 pages)

The book of Revelation reveals a powerful global movement just prior to the return of Christ—a moment which is deeply riveted in both politics and religion. They provide evidence that the Papacy is the religious backbone of this movement as it postures to become the superpower upon the planet. They explain the reason why this globalism will lead to the greatest tyranny this planet has ever witnessed and how every major unit of society will continue to support this globalism. The authors present evidence from biblical prophecy that this global thrust will not completely be achieved and how the world will be liberated from ruthless globalists.

The Evangelical Dilemma (222 pages)

There has never been a more urgent time for an honest review of the past, present and future of Evangelical Protestantism. The authors present an examination of the major doctrinal errors of Evangelical Protestants.

The Everlasting Gospel (368 pages)

This book is written for all sincere Christians of all faiths. The authors have been puzzled why so many Christians strongly believe "the gospel" and yet ignore the central theme of the gospel. The authors have preached this gospel on every inhabited continent of the world and now they present it in a fascinating, simply explained presentation in this book for all to understand and share with others.

Georgia Sits on Grandpa's Knee (R. Standish) (86 pages)

World-traveler Russell Standish delights in visiting with his little grand-daughter, Georgia. She loves to sit on her grandpa's knee and hear stories of "the old times" when her daddy was a little boy in Australia, Malaysia, Thailand, England, and Singapore. And it is Dr. Standish's delight to also share these tales of a family era now past—the joys of life together in exotic lands. Georgia thinks that other children will enjoy her grandpa's stories. Grandpa hopes so, too!

God's Solution for Depression, Guilt and Mental Illness (235 pages)

This powerful book argues with great persuasiveness that God is interested in every aspect of His created beings and that the perfect answers to man's needs are to be found in the Word of God. The five major sections of the book address the problems of depression, guilt, and mental illness in terms of spiritual issues, therapy, physical factors, developmental factors, and marital issues.

Grandpa, You're Back! (R. Standish) (128 pages)

Pastor Russell Standish again delights and fascinates his granddaughter, Georgia, with stories of his many travels to countries ranging from

South America to such far-flung places as Singapore, Africa, and beyond. These stories should pleasantly awaken the imagination of young readers.

Gwanpa and Nanny's Home (R. Standish and Ella Rankin) (128 pages)

"I am Ella Marie Rankin. I want to tell you about Gwanpa's and Nanny's home. But I have a problem! You see, I'm only three and I haven't yet learned to write. So, my Gwanpa is writing my story for me." So begins a book that Russell Standish wrote for his granddaughter.

Impossible Prophecies Fulfilled **(160 pages)**

The Koran of the Muslims and the writings of the Hindus, Buddhists, Shintoists, Taoists, and the Confucianists are conspicuously devoid of prophetic utterances. In contrast, the Bible has literally hundreds of prophecies. Many of these prophecies are rich in detail, unlike the prophecies of Nostradamus which are mystical and lacking in detail. There are prophecies built on time that are very specific. These prophecies defy the challenges of skeptics, agnostics, atheists, and those who follow non-Christian religions. The authors have chosen some of the most fascinating prophecies and have traced them to their pinpoint accuracy as revealed in history. This book is a must for infidels and Christians alike.

Liberty in the Balance **(285 pages)**

The bloodstained pathway to religious and civil liberty faces its greatest test in 200 years. The United States' Bill of Rights lifted the concept of liberty far beyond the realm of toleration to an inalienable right for all citizens. Yet, for a century and a half, some students of the prophecies of John the Revelator have foretold a time just prior to the return of Christ when these most cherished freedoms will be wrenched from the citizens of the United States, and America will enforce its coercive edicts upon the rest of the world. This book traces the courageous battle for freedom—a battle stained with the lives of many martyrs.

The Lord's Day **(317 pages)**

In his famous encyclical *Dies Domini*, Pope John Paul II commenced with these words, "The Lord's Day—as Sunday was called from apostolic times. . . ." To many Protestants, this was an unexpected and much-approved declaration from the Roman Catholic supreme pontiff. The issue of the apostolic origin of Sunday-worship has often been a contentious one between Roman Catholics and Protestants. This book presents an in-depth examination of the Sabbath in the Scriptures.

Modern Bible Translations Unmasked **(256 pages)**

This fascinating book challenges the reader to consider two very serious problems with modern translations: first, the use of corrupted Greek manuscripts, and second, translational bias. The authors are deeply concerned about the paraphrases and some of the efforts to translate the Bible into colloquial language, but they are also deeply concerned about the more respected translations that are gaining great acceptance in today's society. You will learn how these modern translations are reinforcing false teachings and erroneous gospel presentations.

The Mystery of Death **(144 pages)**

There are those today who believe that the soul is immortal and externally preexisted the body. Pagan or Christian, the opinions vary widely. In this book, the history of these concepts is reviewed and the words of Scripture are investigated for a definitive and unchallengeable answer.

Perils of Ecumenism **(416 pages)**

The march of ecumenism seems unstoppable. From its humble roots after the first World War, with the formation of the Faith and Order Council at Edinburgh University, Scotland, and the Works and Labor Council at Oxford University, England, to the formation of the World Council of Churches in 1948 in Amsterdam, it has gained breathtaking momentum. The authors see the ecumenical movement as very clearly identified in Holy Scriptures as the movement devised by the arch-deceiver to beguile the inhabitants of the world.

The Pope's Letter and Sunday Laws **(116 pages)**

The authors examine the biblical foundations upon which the pope seeks to buttress his apostolic letter, *Dies Domini*. Even the undoubted skill of the pope and his scholarly advisors cannot mask the fallacies of the pope's conclusions. The authors show emphatically that the pope's assertions are in deep contradiction to the record of the Holy Bible and that of history.

Postmodernism and the Decline of Christianity **(160 pages)**

Like stealth in the night, postmodernism has not only invaded the world but the church. It is a concept in which there are no universal laws, no ultimates, no immutables. It is a belief which developed out of the modernist world, though it has gone far beyond modernism. Its "truths" are based upon the feelings and whims of each individual. Few Christians have understood the postmodernist agenda, let alone the profound influence it has exerted upon the Christian church. This book exposes how far this influence has invaded the portals of Christian establishments and how it is destroying the very fabric of society.

The Rapture and the Antichrist **(288 pages)**

This book sets forth the plainest truths of Scripture directing Protestantism back to its biblical roots. It will challenge the thinking of all Christians, erase the fictions of the *Left Behind* Series, and plant the reader's spiritual feet firmly on the platform of Scripture.

The Rapture, the End Times and the Millennium **(378 pages)**

This book will open the minds of the readers to a clear understanding of aspects of the end time which have led to much perplexity among lay people and theologians alike. It is also guaranteed to dispel many of the perplexities presently confronting those who are searching for a clear biblical exposition of the last cataclysmic days in which we now live.

The Second Coming **(80 pages)**

The Apostle Paul refers to the second coming of Jesus as the blessed hope. (Titus 2:12) Yet, soon after the death of all the apostles, doubts and debates robbed the people of this assurance and brought in the pagan notion of immediate life after death. In this work, Colin and Russell Standish present a "wake-up call" for every complacent Christian.

Two Beasts, Three Deadly Wounds and Fifteen Popes (334 pages)

Revelation 13 presents two incomprehensible beasts—one of which received a deadly wound in one of its heads. Prophecy stated that this mortal injury would be healed, and that the power represented by the beast would be admired worldwide. The authors give a detailed history of the fifteen popes who have sat upon the papal throne since the infliction of the deadly wound. The reader will find compelling evidence that the deadly wound is now so well healed that there remains virtually no trace of the scar. For students of Scripture, this book will enlighten and bring an understanding of biblical prophecy and perhaps a new appreciation of the conclusive accuracy of Bible prophecy. The authors present this book as for all minds, a challenge to all hearts, and a timely wake-up call for humanity.

The Vision and God's Providences (C. Standish) (176 pages)

The story of the development of Hartland Institute must be attributed to God alone. Yet, many men and women have had the privilege of being His humble instruments to contribute to Hartland's establishment. This book recalls divine leadings, human weakness, misunderstandings, and strong differences of opinion, and we cannot but wonder what God might have accomplished had we listened perfectly to His voice.

Youth, Are You Preparing for Your Divorce? (168 pages)

A majority of youth, including Christian youth, are destined for divorce. Yes, you read this correctly! Unbeknown to them or to their parents, long before marriage or even courtship, the seeds of divorce have been sown to later produce their baneful consequences. Many youth who think they are preparing for marital bliss are preparing for divorce, and, all too frequently, their parents are co-conspirators in this tragedy. The authors provide simple principles to avert the likelihood of future divorce.

Youth Do You Dare! **(C. Standish) (88 pages)**

If you are a young person looking for workable answers to the many issues that confront you today, this book is for you. It presents a call to young people to follow truth and righteousness and to live morally upright lives.

Other Books from Hartland Publications

Behold the Lamb—**David Kang (107 pages)**

God's plan of redemption for this world and the preservation of the universe is revealed in the sanctuary which God constructed through Moses. This book explains the sanctuary service in the light of the Christian's personal experience. Why this book? Because Jesus is coming soon!

Christ and Antichrist—**Samuel J. Cassels (348 pages)**

First published in 1846 by a well-known Presbyterian minister, who called this book "not sectarian, but a Christian and Protestant work." He hoped that the removal of obstacles might result in a more rapid spread of the Gospel. One of these obstacles he saw as "Antichristianity," a term he that he used to describe the Papal system.

Distinctive Vegetarian Cuisine—**Sue M. Weir (326 pages)**

One hundred percent vegan cooking, with no animal products—no meat, milk, eggs, cheese, or even honey. No irritating spices or condiments are used. Most of the ingredients can be found at your local market. Includes additional nutritional information and helpful hints. Make your dinner table appealing to the appetite!

Food for Thought—**Susan Jen (159 pages)**

Where does the energy which food creates come from? What kinds of foods are the most conducive to robust health and well being in all dimensions of our life? What is a balanced diet? Written by a health-care professional, this book examines the food we prepare for our table.

Group Think—Horace E. Walsh (96 pages)

Find out how a state of groupthink (or group dynamics) has often contributed to disaster in secular and spiritual matters, like the role of Hebrew groupthink in the rejection and ultimate crucifixion of the Son of God. See how groupthink is helping the ecumenical movement unite the minds of dedicated men so much that their passion is to build one great super church following Rome.

Heroes of the Reformation—Hagstotz and Hagstotz (307 pages)

This volume brings together a comprehensive picture of the leaders of the Reformation who arose all over Europe. The authors of this volume have made a sincere endeavor to rekindle the spirit of Protestantism in the hearts of this generation.

The History of Protestantism—J. A. Wylie (2,136 pages)

This book pulls back the divine curtain and reveals God's hand in the affairs of His church during the Protestant Reformation. Your heart will be stirred by the lives of Protestant heroes, and your mind captivated by God's simple means to counteract the intrigues of its enemies. As God's church faces the last days, this compelling book will appeal and will be a blessing to adults as well as children.

History of the Reformation of the 16th Century—J. d'Aubigné (1,472 pages)

In history and in prophecy, the Word of God portrays the long-continued conflict between truth and error. Today, we see an alarming lack of understanding in the Protestant church concerning the cause and effect of the Reformation. This reprinted masterpiece pulls back the curtain of history and divine providence to reveal the true catalyst for the Reformation—God's Word and His Holy Spirit.

History of the Reformation in the Time of Calvin—d'Aubigné (2,039 pages)

The renovation of the individual, of the church, and of the human race, is the theme of this work. This renovation is, at the same time, an enfranchisement; and we might assign, as a motto to the Reformation accomplished by Calvin, as well as to apostolic Christianity itself, these words of Jesus Christ: "The truth shall make you free." (John 8:32)

The Method of Grace—John Flavel (458 pages)

In this faithful reprint, John Flavel thoroughly outlines the work of God's Spirit in applying the redemptive work of Christ to the believer. Readers will find their faith challenged and enriched. In true Puritan tradition, a clearly defined theology is delivered with evangelistic fervor by an author urgently concerned about the eternal destiny of the human soul.

The Reformation in Spain—Thomas M'Crie (272 pages)

The boldness with which Luther attacked the abuses and the authority of the church in Rome in the sixteenth century attracted attention throughout Christendom. Luther's writings, along with the earlier ones of Erasmus, gained a foothold with a Spanish people hungry for the truth. Thomas M'Crie makes a case for a Spain free of the religious errors and corruptions that ultimately dried up the resources and poisoned the fountains of a great empire.

Romanism and the Reformation—H. Grattan Guinness (217 pages)

The Reformation of the sixteenth century, which gave birth to Protestantism, was based on Scripture. It gave the Bible back to the world. Such a work of reformation needs to be done again today. The duty of diffusing information on the true character and history of "Romanism and the Reformation" is one that presses on God's faithful people in these days.

Strange Fire—Barry Harker (209 pages)

The Olympic games are almost universally accepted as a great international festival of peace, sportsmanship, and friendly competition. Yet, the games are riddled with conflict, cheating, and objectionable competitiveness. Discover the disturbing truth about the modern Olympics and the role of Christianity in the rise of this neo-pagan religion.

Truth Triumphant—Benjamin George Wilkinson (438 pages)
The prominence given to the "church in the Wilderness" in the Scriptures establishes without argument its existence and emphasizes its importance. The same challenges exist today with the remnant church in its final controversy against the powers of evil to show the holy, unchanging message of the Bible.

Who Are These Three Angels?—Jeff Wehr (126 pages)
The messages of three holy angels unfold for us events that are soon to take place. Their warning is not to be taken lightly. They tell of political and religious movements that signal the soon return of Jesus.

True Education History Series from Hartland Publications

Livingstone: The Pathfinder—Basil Matthews (112 pages)
Like most boys and girls, David Livingstone wondered what he would become when he grew up. He had heard of a brave man who was a missionary doctor in China. He also learned that Dr. Gulztoff had a Hero, Jesus, who had come to people as a healer and missionary. David learned all about this great Physician, he and felt that the finest thing in the whole world for him to do was to follow in the same way and be a medical missionary. That was David's quest, which was his plan. Between these pages, you shall see how God made his good wish come true.

Missionary Annals: Memoir of Robert Moffat—M. L. Wilder (64 pages)
Robert Moffat first heard from his wise and pious mother's lips that there were heathen in the world and of the efforts of Christians sharing the knowledge of a Savior who could raise them out of their base degradation. An intense desire took possession of him to serve God in some marked manner, but he did not know how that would be. Through a series of providential circumstances and in God's good time, the London Society accepted him as one of their missionaries, and in 1816 he embarked on his first trip and got his first glimpse of heathen Africa. Young

and old will be inspired by the many trials, disappointments, triumphs, and wondrous miracles that God can accomplish when one is fully surrendered to Him.

The Waldenses: The Church in the Wilderness—Eulene Borton (68 pages)

The faithful Waldenses in their mountain retreats were married in a spiritual sense to God who promised, "I will betroth thee unto me in faithfulness and thou shalt know the Lord." (Hosea 2:20) No invention of Satan could destroy their union with God. Follow the history of these people as they are compared to the dedicated eagle parents. Illustrated by Joe Maniscalco.

About the Authors

COLIN and RUSSELL STANDISH were born in Newcastle, Australia, in 1933. They both obtained their teaching diplomas from Avondale College in 1951. They were appointed to one-teacher elementary schools in rural areas of New South Wales, each teaching for three years.

In 1958, both completed a major in history and undertook an honors degree in psychology at Sydney University in the field of learning theory. Colin went on to obtain his Master of Arts degree with honors in 1961 and his Doctor of Philosophy in 1964. His Masters Degree in Education was completed in 1967.

Russell graduated as a physician in 1964. Six years later he was admitted to the Royal College of Physicians (UK) by examination. He was elevated to the Fellowship of the Royal Colleges of Physicians in Edinburgh (1983) and Glasgow (1984).

In 1965, Colin was appointed chairman of the education department at Avondale College. Subsequently he held the posts of academic dean and president at West Indies College (1970–1973), chairman of the Department of Psychology, Columbia Union College (1974), president of Columbia Union College (1974–1978), and dean of Weimar College (1978–1983). He was invited to become the foundational president of Hartland Institute (1983–), which comprises a college, a lifestyle center, a publishing house, media services, and a world mission division.

As a consultant physician (internist), Russell held the posts of deputy medical superintendent of the Austin Hospital, University of Melbourne (1975–1978), president of a hospital in Bangkok (1979–1984), medical director at Enton Medical Centre, England (1984–1986), and president of a Penang hospital (1986–1992). From 1992 to the time of his death May 2, 2008, he was speaker and editor for Remnant Herald.

They have co-authored more than forty-five books.

HARTLAND Publications was established in 1984 as a Bible-centered, self-supporting Protestant publishing house. We publish Bible-based books and produce media for Christians of all ages, to help them in the development of their personal characters, always giving glory to God in preparation for the soon return of our Lord and Savior, Christ Jesus. We are especially dedicated to reprinting significant books on Protestant history that might otherwise go out of circulation. Hartland Publications supports and promotes other Christian publishers and media producers who are consistent with biblical principles of truth and righteousness. We are seeking to arouse the spirit of true Protestantism, one that is based on the Bible and the Bible only, thus awakening the world to a sense of the value and privilege of the religious liberty that we currently enjoy.

Office hours (Eastern time):
Monday – Thursday: 9:00 a.m. to 5:00 p.m.
Friday: 9:00 a.m. to 12:00 noon

Payment must be in US dollars by check,
money order, or most credit cards.

You may order via mail, telephone, fax, e-mail, or on our web site:
Hartland Publications
PO Box 1, Rapidan, VA 22733 USA
Order line: 1-800-774-3566 / Fax: 1-540-672-3568
E-mail: sales@hartlandpublications.org
Web site: www.hartlandpublications.com